To John, Paul, George and Ringo for providing the soundtrack of our lives, past, present and future...

ACKNOWLEDGEMENTS

Special thanks with love to Kathy Somach for her tireless efforts in editing, proofing and encouragement.

Thanks to Meg Vosburg, Linda Volpe, the staff at Musicom, Reilly, Emily and Teddy for loving The Beatles and continuing the next generation of Beatles fans.

- Denny Somach

Thanks to my wife Terri Sharp, Mom, Sujata Murthy, Capitol Records, Bill King, Louis Hirshorn, Geoff Hanson, Tim Wargo, Virginia Green (EMI Music, London), David Leaf, Elliot Kendall, Chu Takahashi, Virginia Lohle (Star File), and Michael Lessner.

Special thanks also to Jim Horan for his incredible graphic design, presentation and support, Meredith Musto for additional graphic layout work, Ed Inglis, and Tom Plain, Crystal Lillard, and Alison Ringwall at Bookcrafters.

- Ken Sharp

Denny Somach is President of Musicom International and the former head of Denny Somach Productions, the country's largest independent producer of syndicated radio programming. He is also the executive producer of Eric Johnson's Grammy award winning song "Cliffs Of Dover" and a respected rock historian and collector. Somach, co-author of "Ticket To Ride," an interview compilation celebrating his Beatles' radio program of the same name, lives with his wife Kathleen and three children in Newtown Square, Pennsylvania.

Ken Sharp is a writer/research specialist for a music marketing company. He is also the author of "Overnight Sensation: The Story Of The Raspberries" and is a professional musician/songwriter. He has just released his debut album "1301 Highland Avenue." Sharp lives in a Philadelphia suburb.

Meet
The Beatles...Again!

DENNY SOMACH

KEN SHARP

MUSICOM INTERNATIONAL PUBLISHING

Musicom International Publishing
812 West Darby Road
Havertown, PA 19083

This edition copyright © 1996 Denny Somach Productions
All Rights reserved. No part of this book may be reproduced or utilized in any form or by any means, electronic or mechanical, including photocopying, recording or by any information storage and retrieval system, without prior permission in written form from the publisher and copyright holder.

Library of Congress Cataloging-In-Publication Data: 94-075202

Meet The Beatles…Again/Denny Somach & Ken Sharp
  p. cm.

Printed in the United States of America

Book Design and Production by **Jim Horan** for **TwangBoy Design,** Boston

Front Cover Photo: The Beatles at the launch party for "Sgt. Pepper's Lonely Hearts Club Band," 1967
Courtesy: Pictorial Press Ltd./Star File

Color separations by Unigraphic

TABLE OF CONTENTS

PAUL McCARTNEY	1
LINDA McCARTNEY	15
THE ROLLING STONES	21
DON HENLEY	24
THE WHO	25
GEORGE HARRISON	29
LOUISE HARRISON	42
R.E.M.	51
DAVID BOWIE	53
KISS	55
HOWARD COSELL	57
THE BEACH BOYS	65
ROSANNE CASH	68
THE REMAINS	71
LENNY KRAVITZ	77
ALLAN WILLIAMS & BOB WOOLER	79
THE KINKS	89
THE FOUR SEASONS	91
JACKIE DeSHANNON	95
HARRY NILSSON	98
YOKO ONO	102
JULIAN LENNON	123
BRYAN ADAMS	126
BADFINGER	128
ROGER EBERT	135
HEART	137
GEORGE MARTIN	140
CHEAP TRICK	151

INTRODUCTION

THE BEATLES AT HEATHROW AIRPORT, LONDON, ENGLAND FOR THE TRIP TO AMERICA, FEBRUARY, 1964

PHOTO COURTESY: PICTORIAL PRESS/STAR FILE

*B*elieve it or not, it has been more than thirty years since The Beatles first conquered America. In the wake of the assassination of JFK, the infectious melodies and spellbinding images of those four mop tops from Liverpool, England, provided the spark our nation needed to pull itself out of a somber funk. We all began to live, listen and dance again. The Beatles' profound and unyielding influence continues to shape our collective consciousness and culture today. Before 1964 the word "Beatle" conjured up only the image of a pesky black bug. But, as the innocent sounds of "I Want To Hold Your Hand" and "She Loves You" blared out of radios across our land, the word "Beatle" would forever more elicit visuals of The Fab Four—John Lennon, Paul McCartney, George Harrison and Ringo Starr. Crossing musical genres and changing identities with incomparable ease and consistency, The Beatles were unlike any other rock and roll band; they quite simply transcended the medium to inhabit their own unique stratosphere.

With this exclusive collection of candid conversations with The Beatles and their contemporaries, we salute John, Paul, George and Ringo for their remarkable artistic accomplishments and their equally indelible contributions to our lives and culture as well. We hope after reading Meet The Beatles...Again, you'll pull out a Beatles CD or album and relive those magical Mop Top memories.

And now, please excuse us. It's time for our Beatles break as well!

-Denny Somach and Ken Sharp
September 1996

PAUL McCARTNEY LIVE PHOTO COURTESY: MPL COMMUNICATIONS

PAUL McCARTNEY

ith sales of over one billion records with The Beatles, and countless mega solo hits to his credit, Paul McCartney is the Midas of the music world; everything he touches turns to gold. Acclaimed as the world's most successful pop songwriter of all time, Paul McCartney continues to please and amaze his mighty legion of followers with his astonishing voice and impeccable songcraft. Culled from a variety of press conferences, Paul McCartney addresses topics ranging from when The Beatles met Elvis Presley to his reemergence on the concert trail.

So what brought you back out on the road?

I don't know if it was in the stars or something. I don't think any of us rang each other and said, "Are you coming out?" A friend of mine has a theory that it's the end of the Eighties. One of the influences was Jerry Garcia of the Grateful Dead. His response to that is unmentionable. Seeing the Dead inspired a lot of us. I would bet Mick (Jagger) saw them.

How does your new band differ from the former Wings' line-up?

There are a couple of things different. They're good musicians which is not to say the others weren't. They're all good players, so if we jam we tend to make a halfway decent noise. Certainly The Beatles were good at that. I think the main difference with Wings is that they're very easy going people. We're all older and wiser now. We don't party all night. It's more of a regular crowd than with Wings which was a bit of a party group which is great if you can take the pace.

How did you select the songs to perform on this tour?

I sat down and asked myself what I would like to see "him" play if I was just somebody coming to the show. What I thought I'd like to see the band play. I wrote a list of about thirty-five songs that I consider to be my best songs and we chose from that. Basically we chose from a rock and roll period, pre-Beatles, a Beatles period, Wings period, and then the new album. Interesting about some of The Beatles stuff. I've never actually performed it on-stage. Something like "Sgt. Pepper"...we only recorded that and we never got to do it with The Beatles because we'd stopped touring at that time. I'd get up on stage and say "I've never done this song before." That's nice because they're fresh for me even though they're older songs, never actually done them before.

Do you feel that you have a great deal riding on the tour for you, in terms of re-establishing yourself?

I suppose there's an element of that any time you go out. That's not my prime reason for going out at all. You think about it, the first time we ever went out with The Beatles was risky. We were no one and we had to build the whole thing up. Every time you go out, from time to time you're just not in your hardest period, record wise. I just do my best. Try to go out and play some good music. If people come and see me, great. If they buy the albums, then better.

What goes through your mind when you hear an old Beatles track, one of those 'old chestnuts,' on the radio?

It depends who I'm with and what kind of a mood I'm in. The thought goes through my mind how quickly we recorded all that stuff, mainly. Now you know you'll do a track and they'll do the twelve-inch, and the seven-inch, and the fifteen-inch, and the CD, and cassette and all these crazy versions. I mean we used to go in and in one morning do "Michelle" and then get one little mix on it and it would go on a shelf and that's the only version that exists of it. In the afternoon, we'd knock off "Yesterday" or something. It was real quick how we used to do it. We did our first album in a day, you know.

In terms of songwriting, is it easier or more difficult nowadays as compared to those early, lean years?

If you're lucky, songs are easy to come up with. The magic happens quite quickly. Some of them, you've got to slog out. The ones I feel luckiest with are songs like that. "Put it There" came almost instantly, just over two days while I was on holiday in Zermatt skiing. In the evening I took off those heavy ski boots and went out on the balcony and had a drink and found myself writing. So that one came very quickly. Something like "Yesterday" came out without me knowing it. I just woke up one morning and I kind of dreamed that melody. I was just lucky. I don't really know how that one happened. I haven't got an explanation for that except this idea of a composer being some sort of vehicle that this force flows through.

What prompted you to use your old Hofner Beatle bass again on this tour?

Well, I originally bought it in Hamburg mainly because it was cheap and so was I. I didn't have any money actually. And the other thing is that it was symmetrical...being left-handed I could turn it upside down and it didn't look mad. I haven't played it for a long time 'cause it's kind of a cheap instrument and it doesn't stay in tune easily. But recently I was working with Elvis Costello and he said "Would you play your Hofner please?" And he likes those kind of instruments. So I got it out and started playing it again. And I got to like it again. It's still a nice instrument but it's not as accurate as modern instruments but it's got a really neat tone and stuff.

How does it feel to play your favorite Beatles' songs live... and solo?

It really feels good playing those songs for two reasons. We never really did them that much with The Beatles. "Get Back" we just did in the "Let it Be" film. I made it up during that film and we played it on the roof. It's really nice to get back to those songs 'cause they're fresh for me anyway. I've been doing the other material a lot longer than them. It feels really good to do. The audience likes them. I've seen grown men crying, a lot of emotion. It reminds people of a better time when they were courting each other. It's really good to be the person singing that thing when you see them going through all this stuff. It does take me back.

Any trouble remembering the words to any of the songs?

Yeah. In a way for me it's a bit like a stage play having to remember this play with all these words. I probably get about two or three lines wrong each night. But I call it a different arrangement. I bluff my way out of anything. I always think I know these songs. For instance, when I finished "Hey Jude," I was playing it to John and I got to the bit about "The movement you need is on your shoulder" and said, "Don't worry, we'll change it." He said, "What do you mean, change it...it's brilliant, the best line in the song." The other night I was doing "Hey Jude" and it was very difficult to sing it. I occasionally get a choker. "Put It There" too because it's about my dad and my son. So that gets me and Hamish (Stuart) going a bit.

How has classical music influenced you as a composer?

When I was a kid, I never really listened to classical music. My dad was kind of a jazzer. He used to turn it (classical) off when it came on the radio. When I grew up and started getting into writing music and going to sessions where strings were used and hearing the orchestra rehearse before hand, I really got into it. It was George Martin's suggestion to use a string quartet on "Yesterday." I said, "You're kidding." We sat down and arranged it and put some funny oddball things in it. I went on to do "Eleanor Rigby" and "She's Leaving Home." John did "Walrus" so we messed around quite a bit with those things.

Would you tell us about that much rumoured 1965 summit meeting between The Beatles and Elvis?

It was a great evening. I've heard people have said it was real weird and he was all drugged out and so were we, and it was crazy. It really wasn't. It was a very straight evening. We were major fans of Elvis, particularly his work before he joined the Army. We had a great evening. He was really brilliant. He was the first guy we knew who ever had a remote control on his television. That's how long ago it was. He played "Mohair Sam" all evening on the jukebox, 'cause he was well into that. Priscilla was wheeled in about half past ten for about five minutes as if she was a doll, which she looked like one. It was great. We were totally in awe of him. He was learning to play bass so I kind of taught him a little bit of stuff. A really nice guy, really regular person, what we saw of him.

So, tell us Paul, is there still any good unreleased Beatles material in the vault?

With The Beatles, we always looked at artists like Buddy Holly who, after they died, a lot of stuff came out that was tracks that he had done on his own. We never liked that because it wasn't quite Buddy. So we were very tidy with our material. Anything that we didn't record, we erased or got rid of so there isn't that much outtakes. The best thing in the archives that is unreleased is "Leave My Kitten Alone," an old EMI thing. It's quite a good track worthy of The Beatles. Me, John and George singing harmony on "Three Cool Cats" is quite nice. A lot of the rest of it is just alternate takes that we turned down and they're bringing them back and calling them real interesting takes. They're actually the takes we rejected. They could get a real nice "Gone With The Wind" out of the outtakes probably.

As we talk here in New York City, we imagine that playing the Big Apple must bring back a flood of memories for you.

It's always good memories for me...New York. Plus my wife was born here. It's a great place, <u>the</u> city on earth. I like the people who seem to shoot straight from the shoulder. You get a straight answer. I have lots of memories. I met Ed Sullivan on the street once and he didn't recognize me. (laughs) I said, "Hey Ed, Woooo...I was on your show, man. We got big figures." "Oh, yeah, sure."

What are your views on the current censorship issue clouding and enshrouding the music business?

I think it's a double-edged sword. If you tell kids what not to listen to, that's what they're going to listen to. That's what I was like as a kid. They said to me, "Don't smoke," and I smoked. I think maybe there's a case for kind of saying to certain parents that there's stuff on this record that you may not want your kid to listen to. 'Cause as I say, it can work both ways. They had some programs in England with slightly racy films on late at night. And they used to put a little star in the corner of the screen and that was supposed to mean, "Don't watch this 'cause there's really dirty bits in it!" You used to have to watch the whole damn thing just to see the bit. My main feeling is that to try and ban anything tends to make it more popular.

Undertaking such a strenuous show...over two and a half hours of performing a night...how do you stay in shape?

I used to jog, but then I got a cartilage thing. I now just do the show. Two hours sweating in this kind of heat will do anyone in. It just seems to be something I can do. I feel good doing it and I think that's what keeps me in shape.

Why did you decide to do the John Lennon medley in your show?

We were playing Liverpool and obviously that brings back memories for me particularly of John and the others, but of course with John having died it's different, obviously. So when we got back to Liverpool we were playing to a big crowd like this on the banks of the Mersey. And we decided to do a medley, as it turned out, for John, just as a sort of small tribute really. It just felt so good doing it that we kept it in. It feels really nice to just doff the cap to him because he was a great guy.

What was the idea behind your Russian album and is any release in the offing for America?

There aren't any plans at the moment. People have been asking me about the Russian thing. As you know, it's just available as an import. Which is a strange idea, you know, the Russians are selling the Americans anything. Originally, it was done as a friendship gesture with Reagan and Gorbachev getting it on with their Glasnost and I wanted to be a part of that. We released it for that reason. As to whether it's going to be released over here, I think you'll just have to ask Capitol (Records). I think if enough people want it released, it will be. I'd like to go to Russia. There's every chance of getting over there, particularly now that we've released the album over there and it did well. We looked into doing dates there, but it's the weather. Napoleon and

Hitler both had the same problem. It really is. We opted for Italy 'cause it's just warmer. One of these days we'll get there, when they have a warm spell, we'll be there

Any desire to write your own autobiography?

A couple of years ago I would have definitely said 'no plans,' because I always thought you had to be about sixty-four at least to write an autobiography. What kicked it off was I was at Ringo's wedding and one of the guys, Neil Aspinall, who used to work in Apple, we were talking about something and we both had this memory and the only thing that had changed was the backdrop. He remembered the whole thing at Piccadilly and I at Saville Row. It was very strange. We remembered the exact same thing, only the backdrop had changed completely. So I have actually started to think of writing stuff down just to remind myself. I have written bits and pieces. I wrote twenty thousand words on the Japanese incident, just to really remind myself of what I went through. 'Cause I knew I'd forget, you know. I'd have to read the book myself. For that kind of reason to get the authentic story down as I see it, I'm starting to consider it. And there's also a few dodgy books out, the last few like the Goldman book and a few others, that are very dodgy and they're not based on fact at all.

You're forty-seven now. What are your thoughts on middle age?

I quite like it really. It's not that groovy. I think a lot of people have been encouraged by people like the Grateful Dead. I think there was a time when you thought music equals youth. I don't think it applies anymore. Guys like me or The Rolling Stones will point to people like Muddy Waters and say there's a guy who's seventy and he's still playing and he's still great. We're hoping that it's more in that tradition. I love the fact that people haven't seen us before. I think that's great because I have a lot of young nephews or nieces who say, "Please play 'cause we weren't there the first time around," and I really like that idea. I think a lot of the Sixties stuff anyway is coming back. So it seems like a good time to do that.

What kind of music do you listen to today?

It's so varied, I couldn't really start to tell you so I will. Beach

Boys, a bit of rap, classical music, Sixties music. It really is very varied. That's nothing. I could go right down the list...Otis Redding, reggae. I've got a very varied taste, you know. If music's good, I like it. The list would be really very long of what I listen to.

We've heard that you met the fan featured on the "48 Hours" TV show that spotlighted you on tour.

We did. A lot of people said to me that the bit they loved in that was that girl (Joy Waugh). I hate to tell you that I haven't actually seen it. 'Cause on this tour I'm not looking at reviews cause they always put me off. There's always one line in it that puts me off. So I'm saving them all up 'til the end of July when we get off tour, and I'm gonna read 'em all. We eventually got her (Joy) over to Boston and I met her and her husband and it was great...good fun.

How do you think the music business changed since your days as a Beatle?

There's quite a bit of difference. It was kind of a more intense period with The Beatles. Everything was faster, as I say, we recorded things quicker. John and I used to take about a week to write an album. They'd kind of say, "You've got seven days off, write an album." We'd go, "Okay." And we just did it. We didn't realize you could have said, "We want three months!" like people do now. So it was all just very intense. Like I said, the first album was just one day. Sgt. Pepper was like six months which was supposed to be like "Wow, how can anyone take that long?" And the period of The Beatles from beginning to end was only ten years. People think it was longer than that, but it was only ten years. So it was all much more compressed. It was crazier. Now we seem to have a little more time for things. It takes longer to record things now with the technological advantages around. It takes about a week to switch 'em on.

1993 PRESS CONFERENCE EXCERPTS

One of my favorite songs on the new album "Off The Ground" is "Cosmically Conscious." Does a long version exist? I also heard that it

was written in India.

Yeah, it was. What it is, it's kind of on the end of the record. It's one of those little snippets, you know, almost as an afterthought. There is a full length version and it was written 23 years ago or thereabouts. I think maybe 25, when we were with The Beatles in Rishikesh with the Maharishi and he used to keep saying "be cosmically conscious, peace and joy," so that's pretty much the entire lyrics of that song which is why it's a snippet on the end.

You're doing something as a Patron of the Arts for The Liverpool Institute. What is that?

A few years ago I went back to my old school in Liverpool and found it kind of going to ruins. So I was hoping that something could be done for it because it was built in 1825 and even though I hated it when I went there, like most school kids, couldn't wait to get away. Looking back on it now it was a great experience. It gave me a good footing in the world. What we're gonna hope to do in 1995 is reopen it, renovate it, and reopen it as a performing arts center. For local and overseas. So this is the big dream for 1995.

Does it bother you that critics continue to say that you haven't been able to get rid of that "soft" image? Does that still bother you?

No, not really, no. I mean, there's a lot of people who'd like a soft image, you know. I mean, I don't particularly think I've got a soft image, actually. It depends if you know my work or not. If you know what I've been involved in, then things like "Helter Skelter" is certainly not soft, or "I'm Down" or some of that stuff. So I think anyone who knows me...But maybe I'm known better for songs like "Yesterday," but listen, I'm not knocking it, it's great to be known for both, you know, I'm quite happy with my reputation at the moment.

What's it like being a pop star trying to raise normal kids. And also, I know you're counting the minutes until somebody asked you this, but can you tell us anything about this potential project musical with George Harrison and Ringo Starr?

Yeah, okay...first bit first; the children. The trick is to

remember these questions. The three parter, I'll take the first part...Raising children as a pop star or as anyone famous, me and Linda, when we got together decided that what we'd try and do was raise the kids with their feet on the ground, even though now we're trying to get off the ground. We made that a big priority because we realized that with having money that I have, and the fame, that the kids could become snobs real early, and you see a lot of kids like this, you know, rich kids and stuff, and they're really snotty, you know. So we just decided that we'd send them to the ordinary schools like I went to and give them some good values. I'm really major on that, until they're around 21 and then, forget it, you've got no control over them anyway. But then at least they've got a grounding and the whole thing. And, touch wood, I think that's worked with the kids. They're really nice kids. I mean, I'm biased. But they are good kids, they're sensible and they're not snobs. And what was the second part of this mammoth question?

Your project with George and Ringo.

Oh yeah, well normally when I'm asked this question, "Will The Beatles ever get back together?," we just sorta said "No, it's absolutely impossible anyway, and without John it wouldn't be The Beatles." So that's kind of an easy answer, and it's always been true. But at the moment they're making a ten-part series on The Beatles in England, and it's going very well. We got involved in it, it gives us a chance to say our own point of view rather than everybody speaks for us, you know and says, "You know why he was walking across that crossing with no shoes on?" You know, it's like, "Well, because it was hot." It was like a real hot day and I had sandals on and I kicked them off. You know, big deal, So we're always answering stuff like that. Like I met some kid, little kid who had been to a Beatle summer camp, and she was telling me how you turn the record backwards, and I was saying "No, no, no, I was here..." She said, "No, it's not true!" She wouldn't listen to me. So, it's like we're taking this opportunity with the series to try and put our own point of view. And what happened was we were talking to the director. I was thinking in terms of maybe a montage of John material, say, you know, of him looking great, nice memories of John. I thought, well, you need a piece of music to go with that. So we volunteered to do that. We said, well you know...I kicked it around with the others, "Would you mind doing that? Would we hate to do that? Is that a definite no no?" And George said "Well, that'd be good," and Ringo as well. So we thought, "Well, that's a nice start," rather than trying to get The Beatles back together. There's no touring, we're not thinking of anything like that but we'll probably get together, maybe try and write something, record something for this one piece of music and we'll see just where that takes us. We're not looking to reform The Beatles, but just to get together as friends and make a piece of music would be nice.

A lot of your contemporaries like Eric Clapton and Bob Dylan release box sets of their outtakes, rarities, B-sides. Have you given any thought to that?

Yeah, well that's one of those things that I think will some day happen. What happens with me is I put a new album out, so I'd rather put out new material than outtakes of old material. But I've got a lot of stuff. But originally we were going to for years, going to try and put together and album called "Cold Cuts," which was going to be all the things that didn't get on "Ram," things that didn't get on "Red Rose Speedway," through the years, you know, which I think would be interesting for collectors and for real fans who've got all the other stuff. But as I say when you're going on tour, it becomes a nicer possibility to write new stuff and do that. And plus, "Cold Cuts" is a bootleg, someone's put it together anyway.

When you write music now, are you writing for your fans who grew up listening to you or are you writing for younger fans? And if it's younger fans, how do you stay in touch with the younger generation?

Well, if I do stay in touch with the younger generation, it will be through my kids, because I've got kids of that age, and that's where you get your clues, just watch them, see what they're into, see what's happening. In truth I don't actually write for anyone but myself. I tried, you think, I'll write for the sort of, the moment, or I'll write for the old fans or something. And it's not the way to do it. You shouldn't do anything like that, it's really best to just write for yourself, so that what you care about and what you love comes onto the page or onto the demo or whatever you're doing. And then you take your chances with people, you just hope some young people like it, some older people. So I write for myself really.

Regarding the songs you are going to play... What role do you feel is played in the song writing, the competitiveness?

It was very useful, as you said, if I wrote a good one and played it to him (John) and he'd go right, I'll write one better. Then I'll hear his and I'd think I'll write one better. So it is very handy. In a nice way, we are never vicious. But we are always trying to go one better than each other. But when we came together on songs, then you got a different type of song again. You got things like "I Wanna Hold Your Hand," "Help" and stuff like that. So it was very good, it was very handy to have someone to compete with like that in a friendly way.

As a songwriter, do you find yourself relying on a lot of outside influences?

I get a lot of outside influence, because you just can't help it. You'll be driving along in your car and somebody's got the radio on and that stuff comes in. I absorb that and take what I like out of it. Basically I rely on instincts. Never having been trained, I really don't know how to do this stuff. I wrote my first song when I was 14 and I still approach it the same way each time. It's like magic to me. It's like, "Wow, I wonder if I'll be able to do it today?" I sit down with a little guitar and I'm still amazed when something comes out it looks like a song. And if you are very lucky, you get a special song. Those don't happen all the time, but every so often something comes out that is a little more special. If you keep at it as long as I have, you end up with a few special ones.

It is very unusual to be a left-handed guitar player. Did it ever bother you being left-handed?

My dad gave me a trumpet when I was 14 and I figured out that I couldn't sing with this in my mouth. I asked him if he minded if I traded it in and he said he didn't mind. So I went and traded it in for a guitar. I started to play it the normal, correct way around until I saw a picture of Slim Whitman, who is an old country star. He had his guitar the left-handed way. So I thought there is a hint there. So I turned all the strings around and I could play better because of that. The only time it bothered me was when I was in school and they encouraged me to write with my right hand and I wrote my name starting with the Y, I wrote it backwards. It never bothered me actually. There are quite a lot of people who are left-handed. Leonardo Da Vinci.

Have your children's musical tastes gone one way or the other?

I have always expected my children's musical taste to go directly against mine. And for the generation gap to show up in a big way. You figure it can't go on forever. But it hasn't happened. As you were saying before, I think the young kids now are looking at the Sixties re-examining it. My son for instance is a big fan of Jimi Hendrix. People like James Brown and he is heavy into all that stuff which is great by me because I'm into all that stuff. I love it. I can relate to it all. We don't live in America so he's not into rap. I think he's great. My kids are very supportive. I'm just lucky, they actually like coming to shows. They seem to enjoy the music, it's Dad's music, they support me. The generation gap's never happened in my family, yet.

Doesn't your son play guitar?

Yes, he plays a little bit of guitar. I never really pushed him into it. It's not easy being a famous guy's kid. If any of them are really desperate to get into music, then of course I'll help them, but I'm not going to push them into it. If they just can't stop, then of course I'll help them.

LINDA McCARTNEY

ike Yoko Ono, Linda McCartney has been unfairly savaged by the critics and derided by fans as a "no talent." While she's never professed to be a musical virtuoso, Linda is an indispensable part of Paul McCartney's live shows. Now celebrating over twenty-four years of wedlock, the union of Paul and Linda McCartney has positively flourished amidst a show business world of crumbling marriages. A talented photographer, dedicated environmentalist, and devout vegetarian, Linda McCartney is a strong willed and talented woman, not content to hide in the shadow of her superstar husband. Before Paul McCartney's opening night show at New York's Madison Square Garden in 1989, we had the pleasure of speaking with the "Cook of The House."

What's the best part of touring for you?

Funny you should ask that! (laughs) The best part of touring is the show. And probably the only good part of touring is the show. In fact, definitely that's the only one.

Is it more civilized now, a less hectic pace?

Well, I don't know. I'm a bit jaded, I suppose now. Yeah, it's more civilized yet not civilized 'cause the world is walking around wearing fur coats and I don't think that's very civilized. No, it brought back to me...you know, I'm a great animal lover and I'm sort of amazed how backward America is as far as wearing animal skins. In Britain, there's something called LYNX, which is the anti-fur campaign, and they've made people aware in a very positive way, not like putting their backs up but by getting them to be kind to animals. So I'm amazed to come to these cities that I lived in...I lived in New York almost twenty-five years ago...and it hasn't changed much at all. It's still women with money, older women and some of their daughters who haven't got the message, walking around in these rich coats.

We wanted to go back to 1972 and your first live performance with Wings, the college gigs. Was that a nerve-wracking experience?

Very nerve-wracking in the beginning. Not 'cause of who I was playing with. I think that probably was something that never entered my mind. It was nerve wracking 'cause I was just learning keyboards, whereas now, I can play a twelve-bar or whatever. But then it was like "Oh my God!" 'Cause Paul said, "Let's put a group together," and I said, "Well, I don't really play," and he said, "Well, here's middle C, you can be keyboard player." And then the whole world fell on top of my head! Luckily, I don't care about that stuff. Yeah, now I'm just more experienced and not as innocent. I liked the fact I was more innocent then, definitely, 'cause I really didn't care at all.

In your relationship with Paul, you have the husband and wife, and father and mother, but then there's the musical side as well. How do you balance that?

You know, people are not easy. We're not easy things. Especially parents. I mean, I'm a parent now. It feels weird, 'cause I still feel like the kid, you know? Some days are great and other days the pressures do get to you. And the pressure is always the false pressure. There are things that you let bug you that, really, if you're out in a field with some fresh air, you think, "Oh, that doesn't matter one bit."

The first album you co-wrote songs with Paul on was "Ram." Could you talk about your recollections of making that record and diving into the creative process? Did that come easy for you?

I think it was more natural in the beginning 'cause, again, I hadn't been burned, and after a while you think, "Oh well I won't put my hand in the fire anymore." But "Ram" was total innocence. And that's what I liked about it. People would say, "How could you play with Paul McCartney? You're not a trained musician." Paul McCartney wasn't a trained musician! And I don't like trained music. I've never been a fan of classical music, although my father played it all through my childhood. I've always been rhythm and blues and rock n' roll and, I mean, it's a couple of chords. If you have a good attitude, it's all down to the freedom of it.

You're a strong advocate of environmental issues and vegetarianism. What prompted your interest in that?

As a kid, I grew up in a suburb of New York...and I was well into nature and I was an animal freak, to a point where my parents, who didn't care about animals or know of animals, thought there was something a bit odd. 'Cause I liked animals...not better than people, I just loved watching and being with animals. I used to cry when the horse fell down in the Western, not when the cowboy got shot, which my father used to get really...didn't like that, you know? But I never associated the fact that I used to save carrots to go on weekends to go ride horses at the stables and yet my parents were feeding our dogs horse meat. So there was that...I never thought twice. And, really, I never thought about...I took nature for granted. I loved it with a passion but I never thought what people did to it. And I took animals for granted, because I ate them. I ate ribs and I ate legs, and I ate wings and I ate hearts that they chopped up in gravy, and fried livers. And I never associated that with pain and horror...like Hitler did to people, we're doing to animals. Only they can't speak. And look how long it took to stop Hitler, over ten years or whatever. And all of a sudden, it was Paul, really. We associated the two together, because for the first time when I married Paul, I got to live on a farm, 'cause he had a farm in Scotland he never went to, but I went there and went, "Wow, I like this." So he got into it. And he had sheep when he bought the farm, and the farmer next door took care of the sheep, and every spring they'd separate the boys, they'd cut off their balls and then they'd go in slatted trucks to get their little bodies killed and murdered. And I never thought about it until the farmer came up and he's sort of sorting them out and we thought, "Bloody hell, we eat their legs...we have sheep, we don't even need the money and we're sending them off to the market!" So that's when I became aware.

You recently celebrated your twentieth anniversary of marriage to Paul.

Aaaaaah!

It must be tougher, a showbiz marriage. We're curious...what advice would you give to a couple with marital or career problems?

(laughs) Well, you never know what tomorrow might bring, by the way, so you know, life is hard, and it's hard between people. And you just never know. I don't know what my future's going to be. But as far as it goes, make sure when you...oh, I don't know, 'cause I'm so imperfect myself...just make sure when you do get married...'cause it's easy to go into a store and buy a lot of things; it's hard to get out without paying...so make sure you really care a lot about the person you're with, and be tolerant. I think women have a rough deal. I'm not a feminist per se, but I think women, because they're physically weaker, men dominate them. And like you said, business and pleasure, well, I'm for pleasure myself, so when the businessman comes home and he didn't have a good day at work, you know, and the women just sort of take it. I think there has to be some kind of rapport and understanding. And go vegetarian, I think. 'Cause two vegetarians in the family is so kind, it's just a kinder life. And then your kids grow up in a more modern way.

You were a close follower of the rock scene in the Sixties, taking pictures and being involved when it was really happening. What are your thoughts now, with The Rolling Stones touring, The Who regrouping, Paul on and off the road? What do you attribute this collective longevity to?

I think once a musician or songwriter, always so. It's like Picasso was ninety and he was still painting, and like Country and Rhythm 'n Blues bands, they're not a young people's thing, although a lot of people think it is and journalists talk like this. Music is ageless. And creativity is ageless. I mean, the Sixties were vital but punk in England was vital. I think anything young is vital. And then to keep on means you're really interested. A lot of groups just don't bother after a while. The Stones, I think, they pretty much went on tour for the money. And The Who...and I love Pete Townshend and I loved Moonie (Keith Moon) when he was around...but, you know, the Who aren't really The Who anymore, and they got together because they were The Who.

And the Stones had Brian Jones. I mean, I'm only talking because I was there. I think Paul's on the road 'cause he loves it, and the musicians that he's put together in this band love music. But he's got a lot to follow. He's got a lot of weight from a lot of generations that he's carrying around with him.

You mentioned Pete Townshend. He said in an interview about a year ago that he'd love to see a solo album from you! And we heard that you were working on something with Christine McVie. Would you actually consider that?

It's funny. I've considered it and I've made a few records with different people and record companies, good ones, have been interested. And then I started thinking...well, first of all, I'm married and I've got a lot of kids, so you're talking about how do you keep your marriage going? Well, here I am, I'm going off to Birmingham to promote my record, and then I'm going to do a video, and then do a bit of this...and I started thinking, in the end, why do that? I'm married to somebody who does that. But, recently, I've started writing songs with Susan Harris who wrote "Soap" and "Golden Girls." She's a poignant comedy writer. I've been writing with the British version (of her), a woman in Britain (Carla Lane) who writes good poignant things. Really, animal rights songs and stuff. I mean, I love punk, I love raw music. And I know what Pete (Townshend) means 'cause I've known Pete since way back when and he's great. And he knows. It's funny. I just don't know if, in the life I'm leading, I could do it. I went through a period where I was definitely going to do it. But I've lost a bit of the innocence.

Which song of your husband's do you feel the closest to, on a personal level? We know there are songs like "Lovely Linda" and we've heard there's a song called "Lindiana."

Yeah, that's a nice song. Well, one is "My Love," 'cause I know he wrote that one with me in mind. A lot of "Band On The Run" I feel very associated with because it was such an adventure, and there were just the three of us...me, Denny and Paul...and we all, it's the one album where I played on the basic track before the overdubbing on every single thing, so I got a feeling of being in a "Band On The Run." But I guess "My Love." I love a song called "Daytime Nighttime Suffering," which is a B-side to "Goodnight Tonight," which we wanted to be a single, and the record company didn't want it to be a single, and then we gave them "Goodnight Tonight," and they said, "Well, that's not a single either," and we said, "Well stuff you, it's going to be a single." But "Daytime Nighttime," I think, would have been a smash.

We know Paul likes that as well; it's one of his favorite Wings songs.

Well he might like it 'cause I'm always saying how much I like it. (laughs)

In the Sixties, what was your impression of The Beatles when they first came out? We heard that you were more a Stones fan. Is that true?

No. No. I saw The Beatles at Shea Stadium as a photographer. But I've always loved The Beatles' music, and I loved the Stones' music. And I remember buying Sgt. Pepper in England and then coming back and buying tThe Stones' whatever it was, Satanical whatever it was, and loving it, too. I mean, I love them both. I always loved The Beatles. And I hate all this shit about the Rolling Stones are more rock 'n roll than The Beatles, nyeh, nyeh, nyeh...It's the same with Lennon and McCartney. They both were artists. They both had balls. And they both were romantic.

THE ROLLING STONES

THE ROLLING STONES IN HYDE PARK, LONDON, 1965
COURTESY: PICTORIAL PRESS/STAR FILE

*D*ubbed "The World's Greatest Rock and Roll Band," the Rolling Stones, more than thirty years later, are like the Energizer bunny, still going strong. Despite media speculation of an intense and bitter rivalry, The Beatles-Stones relationship was actually quite close and mutually supportive. Keith Richards and Charlie Watts reminisce about The Four Lads from Liverpool.

Tell us how you happened to score your first hit with The Beatles' "I Wanna Be Your Man."

Keith Richards: We were rehearsing in some little basement club. We had one record out which went top twenty. Reasonable sort of success. There was sort of a buzz going on about the Stones. We'd already met John and Paul and the rest of them. They came down to see us play and saw us even before we made a record. Andrew Oldham, our manager at the time, had previously worked for The Beatles. We were looking for another song because we were going through this period of "okay, now you've recorded all these blues songs, and now what are you gonna do?" Mick and I had never thought of writing songs. We were just about starting to write songs at this time but nothing that the Stones could do. Matter of fact, Marianne Faithfull's record was about to come out..."As Tears Go By"...that was our first song. (laughs) So Andrew had a brainwave, "I know, I'll ask up the old lads, the boys I used to work for." So John and Paul came down to this little club and knocked it off on piano. "You want it, you can have it." "We'll take it!" (laughs)

The press always had a field day with the so-called Beatles-Stones rivalry...did one really exist?

No. It was really all press. Very natural to assume that in a way. Maybe there was a little bit between us. If only that we'd each spur each other on. From that point of view, maybe there was a rivalry. But between ourselves, for instance, we'd check for them if they had a new single to come out and we'd stagger ours. If somebody's was more ready to go, we'd say, "You put yours out first and we'll leave ours for three weeks or a month." It was really a very friendly relationship. Very gentlemanly.

Is it true that George Harrison told Dick Rowe at Decca Records to sign the Stones?

Yeah, it's true. Which was a very shrewd move. Bless his heart, thank you George. Dick Rowe had already turned down The Beatles and here he was being offered another thing by one of The Beatles. You can make one mistake, not two. (laughs)

You've been present at quite a few Beatles' recording sessions, including the infamous "All You Need is Love" free for all. Any recollections?

It was just one mad party. I remember it was just about

everybody in London who made records. "We need a lot of people, so invite anybody you vaguely know." I don't really remember much about it. John and Paul sang on a couple of Stones songs. They're on "Dandelion" and "We Love You." They came over and we sang backups together.

You also played alongside John Lennon in the unreleased Rock and Roll Circus film on The Beatles' song "Yer Blues."

I played bass, yeah. (laughs) That was great. That was the the most bizarre couple of days and it was a long time ago now. The fact that everybody came along and were willing to do things out of the ordinary, especially at that time when the social law of the music business was much stricter than it is now, to be able to get everybody's releases. It's not the first time or the last time I've played with any of them. (Lennon/Clapton/Mitch Mitchell) It was fun to have a little band together for just one number. You won't see that lot together again, that's for sure. (laughs)

Did the publication of John Lennon's first book "In His Own Write" inspire you to do your book "Ode To A High Flying Bird" which was released the same year?

Charlie Watts: Yeah. Well that's why that one was issued because the same guy who issued John Lennon's first book was a guy named Sean O'Mahoney. He used to do a magazine called Beat Monthly and all collectors have them. And because he made lots of money out of this he suddenly thought "Beatles Monthly" and then he did "Stones Monthly," "Rolling Stones Monthly" in those days 'cause he saw a few bob in publishing a book. What he did was...I couldn't get it into the good stores..or so he told me...and he printed up "X" amount, sold them out and it was never heard of for 27 years.(laughs) And now it's been re-released as part of this box set. ("From One Charlie...")

Wow! We didn't know that there was a connection.

Yeah. He did all the magazines. He made a living out of printing magazines and doing stories, fan club magazines they were. And he printed the book. Very nice of him.

DON HENLEY

*ith their soothing yet evocative brand of laid-back Southern California rock and reflection, The Eagles provided the soundtrack for the Seventies generation. Newly reunited after a fourteen year hiatus, we caught up with Eagles' vocalist/drummer Don Henley who offered his take on the Four Lads from Liverpool.*

We've heard that the Fab Four played a pivotal role in your career.

The Beatles are the reason I'm in this business. The first song that I ever sang was a Beatles song, a Paul McCartney song called "She's A Woman." I sang it in someone's living room back in Texas when we were trying to decide who was going to sing in the band. So we had tryouts and that's the song I picked.

Is there a Beatles song that is closest to your heart?

Boy, that's a really hard question. I guess "Yesterday" would be one of my favorite Beatles songs. Gosh, I like all of them.

THE WHO

THE WHO, 1967. LEFT TO RIGHT: KEITH MOON, PETE TOWNSHEND, JOHN ENTWISTLE, AND ROGER DALTREY   COURTESY: PICTORIAL PRESS/STAR FILE

*a*long with The Beatles and The Rolling Stones, The Who stand tall as an integral part of the rock pantheon. Known for their violent stage antics and the passionate and powerful songwriting of Pete Townshend, The Who, recent inductees into The Rock and Roll Hall of Fame, are true music legends. The Who's Pete Townshend, Roger Daltrey and John Entwistle share their memories of John, Paul, George and Ringo.

THE WHO LIVE AT THE PHILADELPHIA SPECTRUM, 1973   PHOTO COURTESY: MICHAEL LESSNER

Didn't The Who open for The Beatles early in their career?

John Entwistle: Yeah, we played with them a couple of times just after they made the "Hard Day's Night" film. We ended up in a little Northern seaside town called Blackpool. We were bottom of the bill and they were top of the bill. We couldn't understand why we were setting up this huge amount of equipment for ourselves. When our stuff was taken off they brought out the Beatles stuff, and it was half the size and they were using the theatre's PA system which was diabolical. The little microphones looked like electric shavers. We couldn't understand why they put themselves through such rubbish. I mean there's much better ways of reproducing sound. But I mean we looked up to them and admired them. We played their stuff ever since we first started. Every English band unless they were successful and had their own material to perform, if you played in a pub, you just had to play Beatles stuff because that's what the audience wanted to hear. If they couldn't actually go and see the Beatles, they'd want to hear someone doing their stuff so we used to do it all the time until we actually signed a record contract and got to perform our own stuff.

Can you remember any of The Beatles songs The Who used to perform?

JE: When their first album came out, we played the whole lot. The whole of their first album. "Please Please Me," "I Want To Hold Your Hand," "Twist And Shout." I mean, "Twist And Shout" we had to do five times a night because it was the big song. I was the one who had to sing it as well. I was semi-professional then and I was still working in the income tax office. And I'd turn up to work the next day with absolutely no voice left at all because I'd sung "Twist And Shout" five times. But we still sing it in our act. We've been doing it as an encore, the same way that we used to do it.

Roger, can you share your memories of opening for The Beatles in Blackpool?

Roger Daltrey: Yeah, it was at the Blackpool Opera house and I remember we were going down in the elevator to the stage to open for them and they got in the elevator and we all stood there dumbstruck. I mean literally, "It's them!" (laughs) We did our act and smashed our gear up. This was before we had hit records and the crowd was screaming their heads off even at us, God knows why. (laughs) We came off and they went on and you could not believe the noise. You couldn't hear one note they played. It was just incredible. I was awestruck at the time. I was awestruck with the image because to see someone who's that famous, it was the first time we'd seen anybody famous! (laughs) And to stand in the same elevator as them...I mean we backed the Stones up before but the Stones were

THE WHO LIVE AT THE PHILADELPHIA SPECTRUM, 1973   PHOTO COURTESY: MICHAEL LESSNER

like us. They weren't really famous, they were scumbags, just like us! (laughs) But the Beatles were really famous. I mean they were pretty. It was funny.

Were you close to any of the members of The Beatles?

RD: No, I mean I suppose Paul's the one that I see the most. He's visited my house and things. But you wouldn't call it close, we're friends. I was quite friendly with John in the early days. I got along great with John. He was kind of a man after my own heart who would call a spade a spade. No bull. (laughs)

Pete, what strikes you about The Beatles legacy?

Pete Townshend: I know the Beatles' recording is very interesting and has a lot of secrets and a lot of gossip, particularly if you work at a studio now in London called Air Studios which is probably one of the premier studios over here where Paul McCartney does most of his recording. What you find is that a lot of the guys who work in the studio there that have been through Abbey Road, Geoff Emerick who actually worked on "Sgt. Pepper," he comes out with all these odd little gems of information and you want to scribble them down and sell them to somebody. But in the end, so much went on, so many different fascinating things happened. You know, I suppose one of these days the story will get told. I just read a book by an English writer called Philip Norman and he wrote that famous book called "Shout" about the Beatles. And, you know, I thought I knew all there was to know. And then you read just a regular book that a good researcher put together and he's talked to sort of somebody's uncle and somebody's road manager's friend of a friend and a girlfriend from Hamburg. And the kind of stuff that you realize that happened around a band like the Beatles is just incredible...the history. They had quite a short career, that's the interesting thing as a band, it was a short career.

GEORGE HARRISON AT THE SPECTRUM, PHILADELPHIA, 12/17/74
PHOTO COURTESY: MICHAEL LESSNER

GEORGE HARRISON

ubbed "The Quiet Beatle" by the media during the early days of Beatlemania, in recent years George Harrison has proved to be anything but silent, judging by the phenomenal success of his supergroup "The Traveling Wilburys" and his ever thriving solo career. A remarkable musician, groundbreaking songwriter, film producer, race car enthusiast, gardening buff, and spiritualist, George Harrison is truly a man for all seasons. In this vintage press conference from 1979, George addresses a myriad of topics including his thoughts on his recently released "George Harrison" album, the "Sgt. Pepper" film and the inevitable Beatle reunion questions.

What are your feelings about your new LP?

I feel good about it. I feel happy about it. It seems, you know, the response to it is really nice. I mean, sometimes it's like you can do something and it's like swimming against the tide. You know no matter what you do, it just doesn't have that natural flavor with it whereas with this one it just feels like the timing, everything, the songs, but it's all as if it's just being supported by positive reaction which is very nice.

How have the changes you've gone through with your last LP "33 1/3" affected the new record?

I think what happened between this album and the last album is that everything has been happening nice for me. My life is getting better all the time, and I'm happy, and I think that it's reflected in the music. Also, on this one I decided that...the last couple of albums it became really difficult making these records because if you're writing the tunes, you're singing on them, you produce them and mix them, you know you go crazy, or I do. I don't know if everybody does. But usually like in a group situation you have a few people who all pull together and bounce off ideas together whereas in my situation I have musicians who come in to do the basic tracks then they all split and so all the decisions would be for me and there's a point where you can get at a loss so I decided out front I would work with somebody else. So I prayed to the Lord that he would send me a co-producer and I got a co-producer and that helped a lot, you know, just having somebody else out front even before the record was started. That helps to have some other opinions so that at least when you know you're going crackers you got somebody to tell you.

How did you wind up losing your voice on the "Dark Horse" album?

On the album, there was only the one cut called "Dark Horse" that I was singing with a hoarse voice, and that was because at the time I was rehearsing to go on the road and I was losing my voice very quickly and I hadn't completed the studio version of "Dark Horse." I had almost finished so I decided, well, as I'm gonna do this live with the band, I'll rehearse the band, and also then we'll just do it like a live take of the song, and use that as the album cut but actually I just listened to it the other day and I think it's great. I love it. I wish I could sing like that more often...like Louis Armstrong.

You've been accused of lacking a sense of humor in your work. How do you respond?

Well, it depends on which side of your face you smile, really. That's been a problem for awhile is that people always felt I was the "serious one" but people don't get concepts about people or they put a tag on somebody and, no matter what you do, they seem to think that's what you are, but if you go back through all those albums, or even with The Beatles, it's more like tongue in cheek. If you say a joke and you don't smile, it doesn't mean to say it's not a joke but this album, for example, "Not Guilty," the whole lyric of that is kind of comedy.

Is that song specifically written about Paul McCartney?

No, it's just about that period in 1968. It's a complete joke, the lyrics. In fact, if you go back on all the records, there's a lot of comedy in it. You just have to look for it.

What was your opinion of the "Sgt. Pepper" film?

Well, that got a bit out of hand. On a TV interview in England they said to me, "What do you think of "Sgt. Pepper," the Stigwood film? I said, "Well, I don't know. Everybody tells me it's awful but I haven't seen it." And then they said, "Are they allowed to do all that?" Referring to all The Beatles and side effects. You know the people who do these stage productions. And I said, "I don't think so. You know there are certain laws that protect individuals' rights or name and likeness or whatever they call it in legal terms." And this is what I said on the TV show that the problem is that The Beatles were all so spaced out and over the last few years that nobody would ever get together again. But finally it's all been unraveled and we've all agreed that what we'd do is we'd have a company, somebody in America and it would be their job to license people if there's any merchandising or if there's any licensing to be done for these sort of things. And it would be that company's job so they don't have to bother us all the time. And, at the same time, if anybody is doing anything illegally, it'd be that company's job to also go out and get them. So that's what I said but The Daily Mail turned it into "Oh, George is suing Robert Stigwood..." He's (Stigwood) cool. I'm sure they made up the script. It's their own and they paid their performance right so you know it's OK.

What did you think of the film?

I didn't see it.

Do you plan on seeing it?

Not tonight. Well, I mean, sure, I'm going to have to see it. I'll probably catch it on an airplane somewhere. Everyone keeps telling me it's awful, so why do you want me to see it? I'd rather see the Fab Four.

What do you think about Allen Klein's tax trial in New York?

I didn't even know he was still up there (in New York). I feel sorry for the man, really...he looks miserable always. But maybe for him he likes it. For me, it's miserable if you're always in court.

How much do you think John Belushi's take off in "The Rutles" resembles Allen Klein?

Quite a lot actually. I mean that line was wonderful. "You ask me where the money is. I don't know where the money is. But if you want some, I'll give it to you." I mean, that sort of summed it up.

How do you select your material?

Getting back to the music. That was what I was saying that it was a great help to have someone to work with as another objective point of view. A lot of different musicians say, well, I like that. Generally they play on whatever tunes you give them. And they don't have that much involvement whereas if you're in a band, it's a livelihood or if you have a co-producer, that way you get much more of an idea if you're going off the rails. So in that respect, I wanted a co-producer, somebody to give me a hand for years. It's very important to the selection of somebody because I'm sure a lot of people would come and produce me but you have to live with someone for a long time. It's important not only that musically you see eye to eye but as personalities you get on.

Why don't you collaborate more with people like Gary Wright?

One of my problems as a songwriter has been that John and Paul were always the songwriters and they started out writing together or later when they had their partnership as songwriters. When John wrote it or Paul wrote it, it always said like Lennon-McCartney. But basically two people, again, it's like in prediction, you can bounce off each other. I've always only written on my own except in situations where I've been forced into writing with somebody else like, say, for example, I wrote some tunes with Ringo because he started the tunes and then got stuck so I had to come and help him finish the tunes or like I did with somebody called Doris Troy and that was because I was producing her album and we got to the session and she didn't have any tunes so we had to make them up on the spot. But generally there's been very few cases where I've sat with somebody and tried to write...I'd love to do it if I could get over the initial problem. I'm sure if I sat with somebody like it was suggested...suggested that I try writing some tunes with other people but if you don't already have a relationship with somebody and just to go into a room and sit with them and say, "Hello, jinga, jinga, jinga," not too wise. I'm sure that will happen maybe for an hour or three or a week or something and then once you get into some sort of communication there, it may work out. Or you may end up with a load of rubbish wishing that you'd just stayed on your own. I don't know but I'd like to do that.

Do you have any plans to tour again?

Come back on the road? I don't know. This continual question is always asked. The honest way of saying it, the answer to it honestly at this moment is 'No.' But there's always a fifty-fifty chance. There's always a part of me that has enjoyed that once you get through all the barriers and all this and that. You get a band and there's always great moments when you want to do less of a thing. But basically, I'm not into touring like Eric Clapton, say, a close friend of mine and he's always on the road. And it's like it becomes a sacred thing "Hey, man, I'm on the road." But on the road for a lot of musicians is a way out. It's a way of escaping from the income tax and the bill collectors and the telephone...your mother-in-law...and it is. And in another way, it is good, too.

GEORGE HARRISON LIVE AT THE PHILADELPHIA SPECTRUM, 12/17/74
PHOTO COURTESY: MICHAEL LESSNER

It's entertainment and people need entertainment but, at the same time, it becomes or is like being an alcoholic, being on the road. It's like a workaholic. It has its problems, too. So I'm not a great fan of touring although, at the same time, to try to think of a way to do it, controlled, sanely, because you find the madness overpowers you until it sucks you into it and until in the end, you just become like a demon on this rolling mad tour while everybody else is sitting around crackers and you got pulled into it. Like in '74. I was ready for the broom after that.

Have you entered a new phase in your musical evolution?

I don't know. I'm always entering new phases each day as far as trying to enjoy the moment now. Just to experience the experience deeper. That's the main thing. Is just to remember that we're all here now and that we're all happy and, if we're not, to try and be happier. And that's the most important thing, no matter what you're doing. I don't think you get happy by going on tour or by coming off tour. I don't see it as this phase or that phase. The phase is to try to manifest love in your life. And that's all, that's really all I can try and do.

Are there deeper meanings in your music?

I think there has always been that element, music has not been just a beat to it. But it's the same with art. There are paintings for you to sit and to enjoy as well as to go into deep and understand the meaning and all that. And I think it's the same with all types of situations. And I think there's a time when you do this and a time when you don't do it. In the early Seventies or Sixties, The Beatles had a lot to say and tell everybody else and me too as a solo artist in the early Seventies and now it's a recurring thing but what I'm trying to say is that try and be happier, that's all, you know. And that's the only thing I'm trying to say. If you push "My Sweet Lord" down people's throats too much, they jump back and try to bite you. And in a way, that message has become a bit more subtle. "Your Love is Forever" on the new album is just really saying the same old story. It's "My Sweet Lord," really. It's just done in a way which maybe is less offensive to people or through me getting a bit older. And you know just being a bit more laid back.

Have you heard of "Come Back Beatles" by The People on Zebra Records?

Nope. I haven't. The last thing I heard was some guy in San Francisco who had this project to reunite John, Paul, George and Ringo. As I wrote to him, I don't know what the others did, because he said if I don't hear from any of you by such and such a date, I'll take it it's free to go ahead with it. And he had all the stationery and the letterhead and all that and all I could say to that was, "Look, that was then." There is this thing that says one of the main problems in life comes from everybody encroaching upon other people's lives. And that's true. You see one country suddenly jump on another country's territory and you have a big war. And I think that's the problem, is when somebody starts out, "Hey, you, I'm coming into your life now to tell you what you should do." Well, the answer to that is, you know, he's on a trip; this guy is on a trip about The Beatles. He's built up this big fantasy about how The Beatles are the only thing that can save the world. And that is complete rubbish. You know, The Beatles can't save the world. We'll be lucky if we can save ourselves.

Do you think a big new group can escape the tag of being 'The New Beatles'?

Somebody who is the New Beatles or the New Bob Dylan or the New Elvis Presley will be whoever he is. It's all the people who don't quite fulfill the public's demands or desires or hopes. They're the ones who get tagged with "They're not the New Beatles or the New Bob Dylan." Bob Dylan is Bob Dylan and The Beatles are The Beatles and when the new one comes along, they'll be whoever they are and you'll never have to ask the question, "When are they coming?" Because The Beatles came when they came. You knew it. The same with Bob Dylan. They'll answer the question just by being there.

Do you think music has stagnated, thus sparking an interest in a return to the Sixties?

Yeah, although I hope that the Eighties would turn into or at least have the spirit that the Sixties created because it was that desire musically to have more intrigue, deeper meaning, generate more love. And we went out of our way. That whole generation. That period. I was very disappointed when it got to like 1969 and suddenly everybody starts kicking each other and stabbing each other in the back again, after the whole 'Love Generation.' Where did they go? Where are you? Suddenly it becomes all this hate and deceit and all that sort of thing so I hope the Eighties, because the Seventies was a bit stagnant and a bit lost in direction and it was this fad, that fad, and it was chopping and changing and I don't know what's in store but I hope, as your questions indicate, there is possibly that desire again to have some positive music.

Did The Beatles lead the media in the Sixties?

Well, I think the media, of course, you are the media and you all know how much you will decide and go after a certain thing if it's of new value, and also to the extent of how much you make a thing news value. That happened with The Beatles and it happens with anything. There is a point where they think, "Good, that's a new tip for the papers" or "That's something new and different to write about." And they go after it and it gets to the point where "OK, now what can we do, we've said everything about it. The only thing we can do is knock it." That's what happened to The Beatles, too, because although everybody talks about The Beatles as being loved, we were loved for one minute and then they hated our guts, then they loved us again, then they hated us, and that was probably one reason why we all went into meditation because, as Maharishi Mahesh Yogi said, it's like you being a little cork, like being a ship on the ocean at the mercy of whatever chopping and changing occurs unless you're anchored to the bottom. And that's what was happening to us. One minute they were patting us on the back. And the next minute, they were stabbing us in the back, and so the point is that we learned you can't rely upon this external change that's happening, just to realize that it is a change and you have to then find some real point. I just had to. So I don't know what the original question was, but the media, you know, how much you create the interest. Maybe there's nothing interesting so you go out and say "Ah, well, we'll go talk to George Harrison. That'll fill the gap until something good comes along." You know how everybody gets sucked into something they can't help but write about. You know to what extent you yourselves day by day...write an article because it demands that you do or because your editor demands that you do or because society demands that you do. I really can't tell. But I think things have a snowballing effect. You know once it gets to a certain point you know someone else kicks in...It's like what happened to Pete Frampton in the early Seventies or Fleetwood Mac or The Bee Gees. It's like in the record business. You can struggle to sell maybe half a million records or a million. You get to a point where if you can get over that normal sales thing until suddenly they are selling six million. I just wish The Beatles had been selling records in the Seventies.

Were you distraught when The Beatles broke up, like Paul says he was?

No. I thought, "Thank God." Not completely. I understand what he means. It was the same like, say, when our business manager, Brian Epstein, died. It was suddenly being faced with the realization that hey, nobody thought that we haven't got that side covered. "What are we going to do?" The idea of The Beatles being like a job, getting off at five and then the factory burns down. For me, I was sort of glad we burned it down. It became too stifling. If you can imagine if any of you've got brothers and sisters and you've grown up and you're all forty years old and you still haven't moved out. It was like that. You need your space. We had to try to help break that Beatle madness in order to have space to breathe, to become sort of human.

Was it that gloomy for you and would you ever consider a Beatles reunion?

It's not gloomy. It's just that it wasn't as much fun for us in the end as it was for all of you. I've said a hundred times what was happening was that we were relatively four sane people going on in the world and everybody else was going crackers. They were using us as an excuse to go mad. "Here come The Beatles. Crash! Let's smash up some windows. Rip up limousines. Just let's have fun and go mad!" And we were in the middle of it all getting the blame.

Does it bother you that people want a Beatles reunion?

Well, I don't know. I did resent it for awhile but not any more. Now I face it. I must admit, it was a privilege to have that experience, to have been one of The Fab Four because there were only four of us who had that experience. Now I don't resent it. I look on it like Laurel and Hardy or the Marx Brothers or anything like that and think it was funny. But it was that time, that period in history. It'll always be there. You can always go and look at the Marx Brothers movies. You can get fed up with it but at least now I can deal with it on a sort of happier level. There was a period of years when it drove me crackers. I would say, "Why don't you shut up asking those dumb questions about The Beatles?" But now it's like, OK.

Do you ever foresee a time when The Beatles would actually reunite?

Just a cup of tea together? To get the four people together and just put them in a room and have tea and satellite it all over the world and charge twenty dollars each to watch it. We could make a fortune. What we could do is just sit there. "Well, John what have you been doing? Well, Ringo I think..." But that would be just as difficult because everybody's left home and they're living their own lives. I haven't seen John for two or three years.

Are you past all the bad feelings?

Oh, sure, everybody's cool now. We could all hang out together and have a great time but the only thing that would spoil it would be all of you with the cameras and microphones.

Will it ever happen?

I doubt it and, if it does, we won't tell you...

On a hypothetical level, what would a reunion album be like? Would it consist of a bunch of songs by each member?

There's a good chance of that. It's all day dreams. Until it ever happens, if it did happen, and I'm telling you it won't, then you'll never know what it would be like. If it did happen, there's no way we'd do a mediocre album. It would be very, very good. Maybe that's what people want. Maybe people want them to all get together and they all fall over and everyone can say, "Yeah, well, I told you they would."

Are you irritated by constantly being asked Beatle reunion questions?

There's a limit to how many times you ought to answer the question. It doesn't bother me once every blue moon or once every time I put an album out, we go through it all again. That's not bad. If it was every day, it would drive me crazy.

★ ★ ★ ★ ★

Out of all the guitar work you've done on record with The Beatles and as a solo artist, what would you cite as your best playing? We love the guitar work on "And Your Bird Can Sing."

Yeah, that was good. That was two of us doubling the part. I'm not sure if it was me and Paul or me and John. But there's two parts in harmony, right. We played them live because everything used to be live because we didn't have enough tracks. Same with things like double-tracking which was the "Nowhere Man" solo. That's double-tracked but we played it together.

Did you use your Fender Strat on that track?

Yeah, it was played on two Strats by John and I.

You underrate yourself as a guitar player. The Chet Atkins-like solo on "All My Loving" is quite tasty.

Yeah, Carl Perkins, Scotty Moore kind of stuff. I don't really know what my best guitar work is. "Cloud Nine,"(laughs) that's pretty good.

LOUISE HARRISON

If it wasn't for George Harrison's eldest sister, Louise, The Beatles might never have succeeded with their British Invasion. Seriously ill at the time of their arrival, Louise nursed George back to health so he could participate in the band's landmark debut appearance on *The Ed Sullivan Show*. A U.S. resident since 1954, Louise rode the surge of Beatlemania on our shores, issuing a highly collectible interview album in 1965 called "All About The Beatles," and doing Beatle reports for eighteen radio stations across America. Today Louise keeps active working with an environmental group called "The Global Village."

At what point did your family recognize George's burgeoning musical talent?

We didn't. (laughs) I was already married and living in Canada when he got his first guitar and started to learn. Mum would write letters to me telling me about his progress and how hard he's practicing to do it, that he was so determined. I think that's one of the traits that we have in our family inherited from both Mum and Dad is total determination. If we put our minds to doing something, we put every ounce of strength and determination and commitment into doing what we want to do.

Do you regret that you weren't living in Liverpool in the early Sixties when The Beatles first became popular?

Oh yeah, it would have been fun to have been there, I'm sure. But I kept in touch with almost everything that was happening because Mum and Dad both, Mum especially was a great letter writer. Even to the fans. From that point of view, it was their friendliness and compassion that started this whole idea of "The Global Family."

Out of all The Beatles' parents, it seems your mother was most excited by their amazing success. She liked to deal with the fans.

She was always very, very friendly and outgoing and fun. Even when I was a very, very small child she used to get a magazine called "The Woman's Companion" and this magazine had a pen pal section in the back. She had pen pals all over the world. Even then. So her reaching out to the rest of the world was part of her nature even before anything ever happened with George.

Did you return to Liverpool at any time while The Beatles were still together?

No. I wasn't there until 1982. I was away from Liverpool from about 1954 until 1982.

Did you keep in touch with George back in their Hamburg days?

Yeah, I had a few letters from George when he was in Hamburg.

Was he a good letter writer?

Yeah, when he was writing letters he was good. (laughs) In fact, back in 1982, I was getting divorced and one of the things that I did at that time was to take to him and give him back all of the letters he had written to me because I was concerned about them falling into the wrong hands. I didn't want them to end up in Sotheby's. So I took everything he'd ever written to me and gave them back to him.

Was he pleased to see his letters again?

Yeah. A couple of days later he said to me, "Reading those letters I realized that we really were having a lot of fun" because all those years later he'd sort of gotten a little bit overwhelmed with the lack of privacy and all of that. The amount of fun that they were having in those earlier days had sort of escaped him.

George visited you in the U.S. in 1963 before The Beatles conquered America.

My brothers George and Peter came over to visit me. They

were here for two weeks. They came to a little town called Benton in Illinois. We went camping a couple of times in The Shawnee Forests. We would go to a little bocce ball club in town. George actually sang at that one, sitting on a stool and playing guitar. A Saturday evening halfway through the vacation, there was a guy in town that I'd met earlier in the year when I first started playing that Beatle album "Please Please Me." I played it all the time, it was great. This one guy who used to deliver stuff to the house would say "What's that music?" He used to come and listen to it every week and he had a little band called "The Four Bests." His name was Gabe McCarty. So he invited George and Pete and my husband and I to come to this gig that he was playing at on a Saturday night. During the evening they persuaded George to come up and do a few songs with them. I will never forget how funny it was because all evening when Gabe and his band were playing he would announce things and everybody was just talking amongst themselves. Nobody was paying any attention. It was in a tiny little town called Eldorado at a VFW hall. There were maybe three hundred people at most there. People were totally ignoring the band. But when the guys asked George to play he got up and started singing the only songs that he knew and that they knew as well. Things like Chuck Berry, and some of the Elvis Presley songs like "Teddy Bear." As soon as he started singing people in the hall started perking up their ears saying, "Wow! What's going on?" They were applauding and stomping on the floor and pounding on the tables. These were very Country type people. They were really going absolutely wild. They had him there and ran through all the songs that they knew how to play together and had him do them twice. (laughs) They didn't want to let him go. I was just like, "Wow! If that's the reaction that one of them can make on his own, then he with the rest of the group must be really fantastic."

When was the first time you saw The Beatles perform live?

It was for The Ed Sullivan Show. Initially George had said he would spend some of his time when he came over to visit me. But then the way everything went with so much hoopla going on that he realized he wasn't going to be allowed to just float around the country at will. So he said, "Why don't you come up and stay with me in New York?" So he booked me at the hotel. First of all, we were going to meet at the airport and he said, "Oh, I think it's going to be a little bit difficult to catch up with each other there." (laughs) So I went to the hotel and he left a message for me with the room number he had booked me in, and the message said to come up to room fourteen, whatever the Presidential Suite they were staying in. So I went up and of course I got stopped by all of the security. So I said, "I'm George Harrison's sister." And they said, "Do you know how many times that's been tried today?" (laughs)

How did you eventually wind up seeing George and the rest of The Beatles?

Well it was a little difficult. George sent word for me to come up and as far as he was concerned that was all I needed. He didn't realize that there are things like security people with lists and you had to have names on lists. Of course, my name wasn't on the list. I had to go through all kinds of things. I had to dig out a photograph that had been taken of me and George. See, my name wasn't Harrison then. It was Caldwell because I was married. I had nothing on me to identify myself as a Harrison except this photograph. It was a Polaroid picture that had been taken in Benton of George and Peter and myself and George is holding my daughter who was three years old in his arms. Then I showed them that and they said, "That looks like one of those guys."

Was George sick then?

No, not at that point. This was on the Friday and then it was later in the evening that he called the hotel doctor.

Was George fearful that he was too sick to appear on The Ed Sullivan Show?

The doctor almost said no, that he couldn't do it because he had one hundred and four temperature. But they pumped him with everything. The doctor wrote down this big list of stuff. He was thinking about getting a nurse to administer the medicine, every hour on the hour. Then the doctor suddenly realized that I was there and was his sister and he said to me, "Would you see to it?" As it turned out, George had a room with two beds in it and Paul and Ringo were sharing another I think. John and Cynthia were sharing another room. So the doctor said, "Would you mind moving in with your brother while we take care of him?" And the doctor said too "It's probably just as well that you're here because I don't think there's a single female in this city that isn't crazy about The Beatles! You'd probably be the only one who could function around him normally." (laughs)

What was it like to meet the rest of The Beatles?

Oh, it was great. They were in the midst of a really great career high. Not using that word in that sense. (laughs) But there had been excitement and jubilance. Every TV in each of the rooms, they had the TV on tuned into different stations and on every station there was something about The Beatles. They were sort of running from room to room watching, saying, "Oh look what they're saying here, look what they're saying here."

You were in the audience for The Ed Sullivan Show. What was that like to witness Beatlemania first hand?

I was just as thrilled about it all as The Beatles themselves. When we went to the Coliseum in Washington, D.C., and I was sitting next to Cynthia (Lennon) and we were both kind of sitting there with goosebumps listening to the tremendous amount of vibrations that were in the theatre. For she and I sitting together to think it's our guys that this all is for was wonderful. I had tears running down my face because it was so overwhelming.

You took the infamous train ride down from New York to Washington.

Oh yeah. The Maysles Brothers, who filmed it all, I'm sure I was in a lot of the footage but I was cut out. I'm sure there is some footage of me with them that I'd love to be able to get hold of it for my kids' sake.

When was the next time you saw George again?

Oh during the 1964 summer tour in several places in America. When I was with them in Washington we went to a big to-do at The British Ambassador's pad. While we were there Ringo got that famous hair cut. But what happened for me when I got back home later that week was one of the radio stations in St. Louis that I'd tried to have them play Beatles music months before, they had this news report on that Lady Ormsby Gore, the Ambassador's wife, had wrestled Ringo to the ground and cut his hair off. I thought "My Goodness." She was a dignified lady who I was sitting with at the same table chatting and I was upset. I was upset that the hoopla about The Beatles was including people like her. So I called the radio station and of course they knew who I was because they had turned me down on playing the records. I said, "Will you please correct that misinformation because that wasn't what happened?" So they asked me to come on the air and correct it. I said, "I don't know. I'm just a little mid-western housewife, I don't want to do that." So they corrected the information and a few days later they called and they said, "You know, there's so much interest in The Beatles and there's so many crazy stories going around about them, you'd be in a position to know what's right and what's not right. Would you be interested in doing some anecdotes about them?" They said they'd pay me seventeen dollars for each one. I was starting to get mail, as my parents did, from all over the world by then. I had sent a letter to a Beatles magazine called "The Beatles Book." George had brought me a couple over when he came in September of '63, I think it was the first copy. I had written a letter to the magazine saying how much I liked it and I just signed it Louise. I had said something about my brother. So I signed it Louise, Benton, Illinois. It didn't have my address. The mail started coming in for Louise, Benton, Illinois from all over the world. I was trying to answer all these letters. So when the guy at the radio station said he'd pay me seventeen dollars for each story and he wanted ten of them a week I thought, "Oh boy, that will cover some of the postage answering these letters." (laughs) I ended up doing them for almost eighteen months on eighteen major stations all across the country. Of course they were AM stations back then. Then they created the Louise Harrison fan club.

In 1965 and 1966 you saw The Beatles perform live in America?

Yeah. See, all of the time they were touring the different radio stations that I was broadcasting for would invite me to come to their city and I would do an hour or so of on-the-air phone in kind of stuff. People would call in and talk to me before the concert. Usually I would do one afterwards to get people's reactions.

It was a good excuse to see your brother.

Exactly.

Was it tough keeping in contact with George during those crazy days of Beatlemania?

No. Not that bad because Mum was the intermediary. In fact, the radio stations set it up so I could call home couple of times a week and charge it to them in order to get the information for The Beatle report so I could keep up to date with what was happening.

What was your impression of The Beatles' manager Brian Epstein?

He was brilliant. I was in touch with him a lot during that first year. Back then you didn't keep copies of what you'd write but I would write twelve, thirteen page letters to him. I was getting 'Cashbox'and 'Billboard' over here and was trying to research the market. They didn't know what was happening over here.

By the way, did you enjoy "The Rutles?" George is a big fan.

Oh yeah, I loved it. All The Beatles and people in Liverpool have a similar sense of humor. There's something very regional about the Liverpudlian sense of humor in as much as largely the biggest part of it is putting ourselves down. We make fun of ourselves first. I've been told by people when I make jokes about myself that I shouldn't knock myself. I say, "I'm not knocking myself. I'm just making a joke," because my self-esteem is fine, but if I say stuff like, "My ugly face is gonna break your camera," it's not because I think I have an ugly face, it's because I'm just joking. That's part of the Liverpudlian humor. So George has that. But then again my parents were also very comical. Even more so than the average Liverpudlian. There was always a lot of joking going on. George was even involved with The Rutles and of course we all liked The Monty Pythons.

Where did you see The Beatles play live?

I went to shows in Boston, Cincinnati, Minneapolis, Kansas City, Jacksonville. I went to a lot of them. I don't remember how many of them because again I didn't keep records. That's one of the problems. People say to me, "You ought to write a book" but I'm too busy living my life to try to write down what I'm doing.

Was it easier to keep in contact with George in the Seventies after The Beatles had disbanded?

Yes. I was living in New York and so I would see him often when he was in New York. He came to visit me at his apartment.

Did you see any of George's live shows on his 1974 U.S. tour?

Yes. It was great. Both of my kids went and saw it too because they were in their teens then.

George has never been a big fan of touring but when he recently embarked on a Japanese tour, were you surprised?

I'm never surprised by anything George does. He was sort of fed up with touring. He turned down the idea of doing it first but then he thought, "Well...why not?" We're all very spontaneous and I think probably all four of The Beatles are kind of spontaneous and very down to earth and very real and fun. That's probably why the whole aura of what they're all about has lasted. They were very real and they weren't predictable.

Is it true you were the one who unfortunately had to tell George about John Lennon's death?

Yeah, but I didn't get through to George. I got through to my brother Harry. I had just gone to bed. It was a very early night for me. I had just turned the TV off and settled down. Somebody called and said to me, "Are you watching TV?" And I said, "No." And there was just something in her voice and immediately I said, "What's happened?" And she said, "John's been shot." I would say that was the most significant time in my life when I had two totally opposite emotions at the same time. One of horror at what I was being told and one of relief that it wasn't George. I've never experienced a moment like that in my life where two totally opposite emotions were instantaneous. So anyway I called Harry at about six o'clock in the morning and then he told George.

Is George a fan of conventions like 'Beatlefest'?

I couldn't really speak about what his attitude is actually. He knows about it. I keep writing him big long letters spelling out everything. In fact, he actually allowed me to use his song "Save The World" to back my PSA's (public service announcements) for our Global Village project. Anywhere where you get a whole bunch of Beatle people together it's always such a good atmosphere and there's a lot of fun. People make life-long friends. It's one thing that's helped link generations together because before The Beatles they were always talking about the generation gap. But now, for people who follow Beatles' music, there's no generation gap in those families because they take their kids to see all The Beatles' tribute bands. I was at one the other week in St. Louis and there was a lady about two rows behind me and she was in her fifties and was there with her daughter and the daughter's child. And this kid was about two years old and she kept shouting out to the guy playing drums, "Ringo, I love you!" (laughs) So it transcends generations.

R.E.M.

L-R: MIKE MILLS, PETER BUCK, MICHAEL STIPE & BILL BERRY
PHOTO COURTESY: ANTON CORBIJN/WARNER BROTHERS RECORDS

The alternative rock band that put Athens, Georgia, on the musical map, R.E.M. is now well into their second decade of committed and compelling artistry. Here R.E.M. guitarist Peter Buck and bassist Mike Mills discuss how The Beatles have served as their musical inspiration.

What kind of impact did the Fab Four have on you during your formative years?

Peter Buck: I listened to them when I was a kid and bought some of their singles and stuff. But I also bought Supremes records and The Monkees, and the Stones and The Beach Boys. I like The Beatles a lot. I really respect their really weird sense of chord changes and harmonies and stuff.

Mike Mills: Their harmonies and their songwriting, I think were the real strong points of The Beatles for me.

Any favorite Beatle songs?

MM: You know I was thinking about The Beatles and on any given day you could ask somebody that and they might name a different song. I think "Rain" is probably my favorite.

PB: I like "Tomorrow Never Knows" just 'cause it's so confusing. I kind of like their mid-period—"Paperback Writer" and stuff.

DAVID BOWIE

DAVID BOWIE LIVE AT THE TOWER THEATRE, PHILADELPHIA   PHOTO COURTESY: MICHAEL LESSNER

a rock pioneer whose colorful and outrageous androgynous image paved the way for the likes of Boy George and The Eurythmics, David Bowie has been an indispensable part of the rock landscape for over twenty-five years. A versatile singer, innovative songwriter, and accomplished live performer, David Bowie captured the imagination of fans worldwide with his fascinating array of alter-images, "Ziggy Stardust," "Aladdin Sane" and "The Thin White Duke," among others. Here David recalls how he came to join forces with John Lennon to co-write one of his biggest hits, "Fame."

Tell us how you came to collaborate with John Lennon on one of your biggest hits, "Fame."

I was living at The Pierre Hotel in New York at the time. I was doing a lot of video experiments—black and white Sony reel to reel—playing around with lots of ideas for little animated ideas. John used to come over. I think he was getting back into drawing because we both sort of used to have drawing conversations where we'd talk and draw and paint, and whatever. I was doing the "Young Americans" album at the time and it inevitably came out that he wanted to come down and hang out for a bit. We were down there one night and Carlos Alomar was playing a riff that we got from an old Flares song called "Footstompin'." John liked it a lot and went into the studio as well with a guitar and started singing "Fame" (sings) over it. That sort of became "Fame."

K I S S

KISS

PHOTO COURTESY: KEN SHARP COLLECTION

With their colorful Kabuki makeup, outrageous costumes, and spectacular stage shows, Kiss are a rock and roll institution. Celebrating their 20th anniversary, Kiss, love 'em or hate 'em, continue to thrive. Kiss' lead vocalist and rhythm guitarist Paul Stanley, whose real name is Stanley Eisen, later legally changed his first name to Paul after his favorite mop top. Here Paul Stanley shares how The Fab Four shaped his musical approach.

Paul, how did The Beatles influence you?

I think that the thing that impressed me the most about The Beatles was that when you saw them you knew the four guys in the band definitely belonged together. Up until then you had bands where there was a short guy, a tall guy, a fat guy. With The Beatles if you walked into a room with one hundred and fifty people you'd pick out those four guys because they had a similar look, a similar style and a similar mentality that somehow worked together. I think when Kiss first got together that's what we wanted, a much more extreme version of a group identity where you saw somebody and you had a feeling and you knew who they were, what they were doing and who else they were playing with.

Do you have any favorite Beatles songs?

"Got To Get You Into My Life" is great. "She Loves You" is great. There's so many great Beatle songs.

Howard Cosell — Photo Courtesy: Vinnie Zuffante/Star File

HOWARD COSELL

Howard Cosell is considered one of the world's foremost television sports personalities. Beyond his expansive, brash and opinionated coverage of football, boxing, and baseball, Cosell flirted with the entertainment field as well. In the early Seventies, Cosell landed John Lennon for his syndicated radio program and began an enduring and unlikely friendship with the former Beatle. Just six years later, Cosell would have the unfortunate task of announcing to the world that John Lennon was dead on ABC's "Monday Night Football."

Do you remember the first time you heard the Beatles' music and how you felt about it? Were you a fan or were your daughters the original Beatle fans?

Well my daughters and my wife were fans of the Beatles. I don't quite remember the first time I got involved with the Beatles, but it was probably when they appeared on the Ed Sullivan Show.

When you saw them that first time on the Ed Sullivan Show, could you sense there was something different about them and that maybe they would catch on?

I didn't, but my daughters and my wife did, and because of them I began to listen more closely, and it was clear they (the Beatles) had a far-reaching and dimensional impact upon the society that was the prevalent society at the time. You have to remember that these were unique times in the country when the Beatles appeared; that it was a devastating age for many people. It was the age of the drug culture, the birth of the pill, the three assassinations with an attempted fourth. Putting it into perspective, it was the age of an enduring and basically unwanted war, and it was the age of maybe the most horrible moment in the history of this country: the shootdown at Kent State. And you put it all together. It was the age of Richard Nixon, it was the age of the betrayal of the presidency, you put all of these things together and in perspective, and it was clear that the Beatles had struck a chord that was far bigger than mere music. And yet somehow the music was expressive.

Indeed it may be that the most important song of the era was not even a Beatles song. It may have been Peter, Paul and Mary's "Blowing in the Wind." That may have been the single piece of music that struck more than any other. But so many Beatles pieces, so many of them, became historic because of their relationship to the time. And yes, the music was great, it touched the nerve center of most of the American people. And John Lennon, I think in particular, regardless of whatever the relationship truly was between John Lennon and Paul McCartney, John Lennon was a genius, and he was also a man who, for whatever reason, became very important to me. I did shows with him. But in his own way, John Lennon became very attached to me and became very interested in Monday Night Football.

Was your first meeting with Lennon on your radio show or was it when he came on Monday Night Football? How did this meeting come about?

John Lennon was brought to me by a fellow named Rick Sklar who at the time ran ABC Radio and made WABC Radio at the time by far the most compelling programming that there was. He brought John Lennon to me and I did a show with John Lennon on ABC Radio Network coast to coast. He loved it and he knew who I was because I was transcendental to sports at that time. Then he said he wanted to go to a Monday night game, and I took him to a Monday night game at Candlestick Park; he happened to have been in California at the time, and I introduced him in the booth to another man who was the exact opposite of John Lennon, it was Governor Ronald Reagan. I used them as the real odd couple.

Subsequently, I took John Lennon to another Monday night game, and then, still subsequently, we met at "21," (the legendary New York restaurant) and we talked and I told John Lennon that I wanted to reunite him with the Beatles. He said it was just not possible. He would love to do it, he said, but call

Ringo, maybe he'll do it. He wrote me and told me it was just impossible, and he wrote me again to call Ringo.

It's interesting that you mention Candlestick Park. That's a historic place for the Beatles for they performed their last concert at that very stadium. How did John get along with Ronald Reagan at the time? Was it just a quick meeting?

Ronald Reagan is Ronald Reagan. He can be charming, and he was. He doesn't have a clue; he didn't have a clue.

When you interviewed John, was he as you expected him to be? What were some of the topics that you discussed? Was he still trying to get his green card? He had a lot of problems with immigration at that time...was that one of the topics?

I didn't go into that kind of thing with John. John knew that I liked him very much, that I thought he was a heavyweight of the highest order and that people reacted to him historically and that's why he loved coming down. Roone Arledge came down to sit with me when I interviewed Lennon. He was in awe of Lennon. He loved him. When John Lennon was killed at the Dakota Apartments, Roone Arledge called me. I was in Miami, Florida, and he said, "Howard, you've got to tell the people that John Lennon is dead." I was shocked, so I opened Monday Night Football that night and talked about John Lennon and his death and how he was a towering figure, a towering artist.

Subsequently, one of my closest friends in life is a man named David Wolper. Right here, right in this room, David Wolper came to see me, together with his director. He was making a movie about John Lennon. He said, "Howard, I have killed myself. I wanted to open the movie with you talking about John Lennon on Monday Night Football, because that's how America learned about the death of John Lennon." Later he said it didn't work. I said, "Don't worry about it, you do it your way." He said, "I just want it to be historically accurate and it didn't work, We could not make it work." I said, "Forget it. I felt very deeply about

John Lennon. You do the picture the right way, because you're a genius. There's nobody in television who can even compete with you." So he had to to it his way.

It is true that most people in the nation heard about John's death through you. You were the first person to bring the news. Was there some hesitation as to just how you would word it? To put it in perspective, obviously a football game is meaningless...how did you handle that? Was that difficult?

I have become in my lifetime the deliverer of eulogies. At St. Patrick's for Roger Maris, for Michael Burke, for Billy Martin, and that's become my lot in life when it comes to sports. When it came to John Lennon, it was natural. I am not a sportscaster, I am a journalist, and I am a man of intellectual dimension. When Roone asked me to open the show with the death of John Lennon, I said that the football game was of no consequence...in essence that's what I said. I said, "One of the great figures of the entire world, one of the great artists, was shot to death horribly at the Dakota Apartments, 72nd Street and Central Park West in New York City. John Lennon is dead. He was the most important member of the Beatles, and the Beatles, led by John Lennon, created music that touched the whole of civilization. Not just people in Liverpool, where the group was born, but the people of the world." And I talked about the music that they had created, the times in which they had all lived and in which John Lennon lived. I related what happened in terms of the music to the social spectrum and the impact upon the entire world.

Let's go back to those radio broadcasts. Did you ever introduce your daughters to John in any of your encounters? Being big fans, were they impressed that Dad interviewed the major member of the Beatles?

Yes. My younger daughter, who's a woman now, recently went to the Garden to see McCartney. She was deeply touched, she said it was like old times. I was very proud of handling the death of John Lennon with an understanding, a sensitivity, and a concern about bringing it home to everybody...the troops overseas, in Weisbaden they would listen to Monday Night Football, and there was a shock, a disbelief that John Lennon had been killed. It was a terrible thing.

As a journalist, would you have any interest in interviewing McCartney, Harrison or Starr?

I'm rather tired of what Paul is doing, because what he's doing is reciting.

Could you open him up?

I don't think so, I think there's a kind of puppetry now. I don't think I could open him up. Ringo...what's Ringo become? Lennon was the cement that made the Beatles, without question.

You spoke earlier about the television show on which you tried to reunite the Beatles. Did that air in the mid Seventies?

That was in 1976 that I did that show for twenty-two weeks, and it was my dream to reunite them all. John just said, "It won't happen, I can't do it." He said, "If there was anybody I would love to do it for, it would be you." Then I said, "Look, if we can't reunite, we can't." He just didn't want to do it.

Who did you get in place of the Beatles? Wasn't it the Bay City Rollers?

The Bay City Rollers, yeah. I did that for Sid Bernstein, who was involved with The Beatles originally. He's a hustling little promoter, Sidney. But the Bay City Rollers, obviously, didn't make it.

Did you ever see the Beatles live, or as solo artists, with your daughters or on your own in a journalistic capacity?

Not with my daughters. I saw the Beatles when I was in the audience at Ed Sullivan.

What was that like? Was there a sense, maybe from the audience, that this was something truly special?

The audience went crazy over the Beatles on the Sullivan show. Sullivan served a purpose with that show for the Beatles.

He launched Elvis, too. It's incredible. He launched two of the greatest musical phenomena of the past thirty years.

"Eleanor Rigby"...everything the Beatles did was historic. They were in their place, in their time.

Is there a Beatles song you feel most personally about, that connects well with you or that you have fond memories of?

I used to kid John Lennon. I would say, "John, there's something in the way you move." He'd get such a kick out of it. I loved John Lennon and he really liked me. I thought he had a sense of life, the pulsation of life, and he loved Yoko Ono and made no apologies for the way he lived, for anything he did.

In your eyes, why do you feel John Lennon's passing, which you announced on Monday Night Football to the world, caused such national grief, like John F. Kennedy? What is it about him that struck a chord?

They brought a whole new sweep to music, the Beatles did, led by John Lennon. They touched a nerve center, a chord in their music for all of the people all over the world. The Beatles knew me. In fact, I held a press conference just the other day in Palm Springs at my golf tournament, and an old dear friend was there, Telly Savalas. Telly and I spent a lot of time together in London with Muhammed Ali. Now Muhammed Ali, by the way, knew who the Beatles were, and he said, "Those people, they're as important as I am." He understood who he was, and he understood who the Beatles were.

The Beatles met him. There are some classic photos of them in 1964.

Sure they did. They knew Muhammed. They knew Muhammed was very important in this society.

And for Muhammed, who had a very high sense of self importance, to say that about the Beatles was definitely something.

Yes, it was.

In your eyes, what was John Lennon's greatest contribution musically, socially and politically? What would you want people to remember about John Lennon?

I think that is reaching too far. I think John Lennon should be remembered as I've described him.

He was a great artist. He was the leader of a young group that changed the world of music throughout this civilization; that his impact resounded throughout the entire world; and that he lived it his way and created music his way. I don't think there is a greater thing to be left to this society than his music, than the way he comported himself, than the understanding of his times and the understanding of people of his time. I think that's overwhelming, and I don't think you should stretch for more. What Lennon did is historic, and I think he was a great force musically to be remembered always.

Thankfully you were involved in a large part of his career.

I was very fortunate, and I still have letters in my files that he wrote to me, and it means a very great deal to me. I've been a very fortunate man to have had people in the course of a lifetime, where my own life intertwined with theirs. So many people have talked to me: "We remember, we learned about John Lennon's death through you." It's a hell of a thing...

THE BEACH BOYS

SITTING: BRUCE JOHNSTON & AL JARDINE, STANDING: BRIAN WILSON, MIKE LOVE & CARL WILSON PHOTO COURTESY: CAPITOL RECORDS

*A*merica's answer to The Beatles, The Beach Boys lived full-tilt the California dream, a dream of unlimited sunshine, surf and a bevy of bikini clad girls. No contemporary rock artist had as profound an influence on The Beatles than The Beach Boys. Whether it was the group's innovative "Pet Sounds" album that inspired The Beatles to create "Sgt. Pepper," The Beatles' Beach Boy's homage on "Back In The USSR," or more specifically, Brian Wilson's Herculean songwriting talent, all had a dramatic effect on John, Paul, George and Ringo. Here Brian and Carl Wilson share their heartfelt memories of the Fab Four, who were always friends, never rivals.

What are your recollections of playing with Ringo Starr on July 4, 1984 in front of over 750,000 people in Washington, D.C.?

Carl Wilson: It was a real thrill to play with him. We had the sound system break down but under all the stuff and the craziness backstage, it was really neat to hear him play. You know, to get down to the essence of him playing and the sound that occurred when he was beating the drums was really something.

How did you get Ringo to play drums on the Beach Boys song "California Calling?"

CW: We just asked him. We were more than friends (with the Beatles). It was more an affinity, sort of an inner relationship like a friendship, buddies, stuff like that. Paul and Linda have been really great to Brian. They've been very caring and loving and they're really good people.

I remember reading a quote from Paul McCartney saying that "God Only Knows" was the perfect pop song.

CW: That was really a beautiful compliment. That's one of those seven minute wonders. Brian just popped it out, it was just a joke how fast it came out.

Brian Wilson: It's a thrill. I get a big thrill out of hearing that. I appreciate his support. I mean he's supporting me when he says that. He's one of my fans. I'd like to work with him. Did you hear the record "The Girl Is Mine" that Paul did with Michael Jackson? Well I'd like to do something like that with Paul McCartney. I'd like to write with him and cut a record.

And it's ironic that "Pet Sounds" inspired the creation of The Beatles' most revered album "Sgt. Pepper."

CW: It was their concept album. They certainly went over the top with it, right? There's some really beautiful things on that. That feeling the first time of hearing Ringo sing "With A Little Help From My Friends" is real powerful in anybody's book. And anybody who was listening to the records that we were at the time and taking all that into consideration, that was really beautiful.

What was Paul's involvement with The Beach Boys song "Vegetables" from the "Smiley Smile" album? It's been rumored that he appears on the song, either playing or munching vegetables.

CW: Oh, he was at the session. And then the rest of us had to leave to go to Europe the next day so I don't really know what happened after that.

BW: McCartney was there at the "Vegetables" session but he was not on the record. He played a song called "She's Leaving Home" on the piano and said, "I wrote this." And that's before they recorded it.

The Beach Boys covered several Beatles songs on your 1965 LP "Party", "I Should Have Known Better," "Tell Me Why," and "You've Got To Hide Your Love Away." What prompted you to do those songs?

BW: We did them simply because Al (Jardine) and Carl liked the Beatles, they liked them a lot.

Was there any sense of competition between The Beatles and The Beach Boys in the Sixties.

BW: It was just sort of like an inner group rivalry thing. They pushed me very hard.

Why are The Beatles still so popular in your eyes?

BW: The way Paul and John looked for one thing. They had a certain kind of haircut for one thing. The way they sounded. God, John Lennon is a great singer! I thought he was the best singer in the group.

Any favorite Beatles songs?

BW: "She's Leaving Home" because he played it for me at the studio one night. I told him, "Paul, this is going to be a big one for you!" And he said, "Thank you Brian."

ROSANNE CASH

ROSANNE CASH PHOTO: MELODIE GIMPLE/COLUMBIA RECORDS

The daughter of Country sensation Johnny Cash, Rosanne Cash's early musical memories weren't colored by the sounds of Country, but rather the rock and roll of The Fab Four. A true-blue first generation Beatles' fan, Rosanne Cash has carved out a formidable career in Country music, tallying a string of hits and gold records. Beatle fans may be familiar with Rosanne through her sparkling cover of The Beatles' "I Don't Want To Spoil The Party," a Number One Country hit. She also took part in the "Carl Perkins and Friends" 1985 HBO TV special performing with the likes of George Harrison and Ringo Starr. Here Rosanne recalls how she she came to be bitten by the Beatles' bug at an early age.

Can you recall the first time you encountered the music of The Beatles?

I have the most vivid image of the first time I heard the Beatles. I was in second grade and I was sitting next to my friend Gretchen in the back seat of a car. And her older sister was driving the car, driving us to school. I'd spent the night at Gretchen's house, I guess. And they turned on the radio and it was "I Want to Hold Your Hand" and Gretchen was talking in my ear and I couldn't listen to her 'cause I was so enraptured with this song. And all I could think was "How do I find that on the radio? When I go home tonight, how do I find that very thing on the radio?" It was so great and I remember watching them on Ed Sullivan too and my mom told my sisters to be quiet 'cause The Beatles were on and I was watching them.

You had a hit with your cover of "I Don't Want To Spoil The Party." Why did you choose to cover that particular Beatles tune?

Rodney (Crowell) and I both came up with the idea because we both love Beatles songs so much. We thought, "Wouldn't it be cool to do a kind of bluegrass jazz version of "I Don't Want To Spoil The Party?"

Any reaction from The Beatles to your version?

My dad (Johnny Cash) is friendly with Paul McCartney and my dad had said that he (Paul) liked it so maybe he sent him a copy. They've been friendly for many years.

How did you get involved with the "Carl Perkins and Friends" TV special which included George Harrison and Ringo Starr?

Well I think Carl asked for me. I've known Carl since I was little. To tell you the truth, I think they wanted a woman on the show and they were trying to find someone who made sense. I mean that not to slight them or say they're sexist or anything, but I think they consciously wanted to balance it.

What was it like to appear with such legends?

Oh my God, it was just like going to another planet! I mean I walked into rehearsal the first day and George Harrison, Ringo Starr, Eric Clapton, and Carl were there and I went "Well this isn't the planet that I usually reside on, this is entirely different." (laughs)

Was George nervous as this was his first live appearance in many years?

He was very nervous. He was very sweet. I had dinner at his house the night before. And he and Carl and Dave Edmunds sat around until 3am and played all these songs. It was just wonderful.

We heard that you had several vivid dreams where John Lennon appeared after his death that eased the heartache and pain of his loss for you.

Well I had several dreams about John after he died. I know this stuff is kind of wacky. I mean he was such a part of our generation and such a part of our collective consciousness that it was devastating to lose him. It was almost like he sacrificed himself for our generation. So I had several dreams after he died. They were mostly about music, just talking about music. I can't remember the specifics.

But we understand that those dreams made you feel better.

Yeah, they did. I didn't get the feeling that he was entirely happy with being gone though in those dreams.

How did they influence you as a writer?

I think the influence was so great that I probably can't define it. It permeated our generation. It's just there. I don't know that any of us who are musicians today or writers today would be as we are without how the Beatles influenced us.

Is there one Beatles song closest to your heart?

There's so many. "Here, There and Everywhere," "In My Life," "No Reply," "A Day in the Life." I mean, God there's so many!

How about particular Beatle albums?

"Beatles '65" I really liked. "Something New" I really liked. Of course, "Sgt. Pepper" was brilliant!

THE REMAINS

THE REMAINS. **PHOTO COURTESY: BARRY TASHIAN**

oston's The Remains epitomize the classic Sixties garage band. Raw-spirited and full of swagger and attitude, The Remains were true rock and roll punks. While the group had limited commercial success in the Sixties, they still remain popular as a cult act today among retro rock aficionados. Band leader and chief songwriter Barry Tashian remembers spending two weeks on the road as The Beatles' opening act on their last concert tour. And their very presence with the so-called mainstream Beatles signaled that The Fab Four were keeping their ears and eyes open to music being created everywhere, even in Barry Tashian's garage.

You first saw The Beatles on Ed Sullivan. Your impressions?

I loved it. I loved The Beatles, I thought they were great. What can I say? Everything they did was great.

They must have influenced you as a songwriter with The Remains.

Yes, they did. They were inspiring to me in letting it be known that musicians could write their own songs. So I'd think of them when I was struggling over a song and thinking if they can do it, so can I.

What Beatle did you most identify with?

I think John probably appealed to me on a spiritual level the most.

What were your initial impressions of the group once meeting them?

They were fantastic, they were friendly. Paul was a little bit shy, he wasn't quite as open as the other three. Ringo was just a regular guy. John was very friendly, he was a very intense guy. I had some real good times sitting around in the hotels and stuff. I probably spent the most time with George. It just seemed for that two weeks or whatever it was, sixteen, seventeen days, we would sit together on the plane and I would visit with him at the hotel. He had the first cassette player I'd ever seen. He had a Phillips cassette player and he had Ravi Shankar in his room. And so we'd go down there and listen to a little bit of raga and talk about stuff, this and that.

Did you meet the Beatles manager Brian Epstein?

Yes. He was a very nice person. He was the one who made the decision to use our sound system for the whole tour.

Wow! Tell us about that.

Well we showed up for the first concert with our sound man in Boston—it was actually called Hanley sound, Bill Hanley and his brother Terry. We would hire them to do our sound at our shows which was something that was new in rock n' roll for local bands to not have their own sound system. We spent some good money, a good portion of everyone of our concerts paying them to just to do an excellent sound system for us, for the vocals. They didn't mike other instruments back then. We just relied on sheer volume. We tried to get the biggest amps we could get and stuff. So when they heard we were doing the Beatles tour they said, "Well we're gonna come and do your sound. You don't have to worry about paying us." 'Cause we weren't being paid a great deal on the Beatles tour.

How much were you paid?

(laughs) Let's say that we almost broke even doing it. So what happened was the first show was in Chicago so the Hanley people showed up with the sound system and drove right on into the stockyards where the show was gonna be set up and everything. Nobody questioned them or anything. We also had a full complement of Fender equipment that came direct to us from the Fender factory in California. The decision was made to nix that because only Vox equipment (The Beatles choice of amplification) would appear on the stage. Then as showtime arrived and the guys in the stockyards, the crew started firing up their public address system which were a bunch of steel horns up in the ceiling a hundred feet above the seats. We were gonna go on first and we wanted to use our own system which had some great Altec speakers set up on the edge of the system. The union guys said "You can't use this stuff". It was a whole power play. The beginning of the first show was actually postponed. It started late because of this. I was not in on what went on, the upshot was that the house system was turned off and The Beatles ended up using our system for the rest of the tour.

The 1966 tour came hot on the heels of the "bigger than Christ" controversy. Could you sense any nervousness in John?

Yeah. He was nervous because I remember the first time I had the nerve to go over and sit down next to him on the plane, he was wearing a white suit and I was just in awe. And I was cooling it and I sat down and said, "How are you, I'm doing okay, how are you?" And he said, "Ask me after Memphis." 'Cause that was really the place where he expected the trouble because that was the farthest south.

That was the only Bible belt city we played. So yeah, he was kind of nervous about it. They had doubled or tripled security in Memphis and as it was, all that happened is that people did throw cherry bombs during the performance.

What was it like opening for such a worldwide sensation?

It was hard. It was very hard. People were milling around a lot. They had come to see The Beatles. A lot of the people that I've met who went to those shows didn't even remember us. But other people in other places, people did. In some of the places, the press the next day, a place like Detroit in particular called us the surprise hit of the show.

How long did you get to play each night?

We played 25 minutes and we did songs from our album. I remember we did "Thank You" and "Why Do I Cry?," I'm sure we did "I'm a Man." We did "Say You're Sorry." Probably "Once Before."

Is it true that The Remains were attempting to blow The Beatles off the stage?

Well we were young and we were gunning, yes. For them, no. We were gunning for success. This we looked at as a kind of make it or break it situation—which it wasn't. Which in our limited perspective it was a make it or break it situation. So we were trying as hard as we could to get noticed, of course. Which we always did. It wasn't just The Beatles tour. Every gig we'd get backstage in the wings, and we'd like put our hands all together like a baseball team, and like "Alright! We're really gonna do it now. Are you ready? Okay, let's go!" And we'd run out and we just put our all and everything into it. I'd always be absolutely exhausted and dripping wet at the end of every show.

You saw The Beatles live on that tour, your opinion?

I watched a few shows. They sounded pretty good. There was a constant din of screaming going on. I made out some songs. I could hear them. I stood near the stage. They were good players, they were just playing their songs like you'd see them in a bar. There was nothing weird or they didn't have any effects or electronics. It was just three guys playing through amplifiers and a drummer.

Did you get to hang out backstage with the group at all?

It was pretty compartmentalized. We were separated backstage before the shows. Really the only times that we spent together were in the airplanes or in the buses or at the hotels. Except for one night in Hollywood where I kind of galavanted around with them all going to visit various stars.

Share your recollections of that evening.

Well I went up to their house, they had a big house in the Hollywood Hills where they were staying at. We were at a hotel. George sent a limo down to pick me up and I was just...I wanted to be near these people. It was a very nice house and we had dinner. And it was a long table and they had about ten people there. David Crosby was there, and their publicity guy Derek Taylor was there. His children. It was a pretty mellow scene. And The Beatles. There weren't any hangers out. Really. But I remember walking down the hall of this house just checking it out and down the end of the hall Ringo was playing pool with somebody. I walked past one room and I looked in and there was John asleep on the bed just kind of like curled up in a little nap. Then after dinner, David Crosby took George and Paul and I over to see some various people like Roger McGuinn—then Jim McGuinn. We went over to see Cass Elliot. She was friendly. Then we went over to see Brian Wilson and Carl Wilson. It was just sitting in their chairs, they had their wives with them. It was just regular, you know, regular couples. They were very quiet.

What did the conversation center on?

They were talking a little bit about music. It was very casual. I think Derek Taylor was there too and he got up and put on a Byrds album at one point and David Crosby got up and like ripped the needle off. And he said, "Don't play that!" (laughs) I guess he was kind of embarassed or something with all these people sitting together to have the Byrds on. I don't know why he should have been, but he was. So that was a great night.

What do you recall about playing Shea Stadium?

Ah yes. Shea Stadium, a glittering evening. They probably had the most lights at that stadium than anywhere. That was a big moment, that was a big crowd. 55,000 people.

How was the sound?

Well the sound was pretty much the same everywhere. (laughs) We didn't really have any monitors. So we had to play with such a volume that if I had to walk across the stage, we each were playing through two Super Beatle amps, piano, bass and guitars, so as I'd walk across the stage I'd walk through these corridors of sound. And when I walked in front of the electric guitar, I couldn't really hear much else. I could be standing right next to the drummer but I was in the guitar corridor. Then I'd take a couple of steps backwards and I'd be in the piano corridor.

Did you take any photos with The Beatles?

I have some photographs our equipment guy, Ed Freeman took of The Beatles on stage and The Remains on stage. The last flight we were on, I got him to take a couple of pictures of George and I sitting next to each other on the plane and they didn't come out. They were underexposed. All you could see was the little lights above the seats. So I never got any pictures together.

Did you have any inkling from The Beatles themselves that this would be their last tour?

Never knew it would be the last tour, no. I remember after the last show after Candlestick Park and we were were flying back to Los Angeles and we were saying goodbye and everything and I remember John said, I said goodbye to him, and he said, "Yeah, if you're ever within 100 miles, say hello because we won't find you." (laughs) That's what he said.

Have you been in contact with any of The Beatles since the '66 tour?

No, never again. I'd like to see them. We spent a couple weeks in pretty friendly terms. I'd love to see 'em.

LENNY KRAVITZ

LENNY KRAVITZ.   PHOTO COURTESY: PER GUSTAFSON/VIRGIN RECORDS

*D*uring his brief recording career, Lenny Kravitz has already set the rock world on its collective ear with his powerfully soulful evocations of peace and love. His genuine affection for The Beatles, and especially John Lennon's solo material, is well-known and puts an indelible stamp on his solo work. Lenny discusses how The Beatles continue to help shape and influence his art.

We've heard that you didn't get into John Lennon as a solo artist until just recently.

That is true. My manager said, "Had you heard the Plastic Ono stuff?" And I didn't know what the Plastic Ono was. And he said, "Well this is the early John Lennon stuff." And I heard it and I just flipped. And he heard "Be" (from Kravitz's debut solo LP "Let Love Rule") and he said it sounds like a Lennon thing. He's God to me as far as music is concerned.

What appealed to you about John Lennon's music?

It was the emotion. I was listening to "Mother" today and it's like at the end when he's singing "Mother, please don't go." It sounds like this little eight-year old kid screaming for his mother to come back. I guess he'd just done primal therapy before he did this album. You could just hear it from his soul. And that's what turns me on the most. Also the fact that he didn't give a damn about all the stuff, he just wanted to make music. He was brilliant. I definitely love him in the Beatles as well but even more afterwards, for me.

Your drum sound on "Let Love Rule" is reminiscent of Ringo Starr.

I love Ringo Starr. People think he can't play drums but nobody can go around the tom toms like him. He's so quirky about it. It's great, man.

ALLAN WILLIAMS & BOB WOOLER

ALLAN WILLIAMS WITH BEATLE FRIENDS **PHOTO COURTESY: BEATLEFAN ARCHIVES**

While their names may not sound familiar to all but the most knowledgeable Beatles' experts, Allan Williams and Bob Wooler loom large in The Beatles' legend. The outspoken Williams was The Beatles' first manager who arranged their Hamburg, Germany club engagement and later shared his experiences in his splendid book "The Man Who Gave The Beatles Away." Bob Wooler served as announcer for all the Fab Four's seminal performances at "The Cavern." We sat down with these two gentlemen for a no-holds barred account of their days with the Four Lads from Liverpool.

Can you recall the first time you saw the Beatles live?

Bob Wooler: The first time I saw them as the Beatles, in fact they were the "Silver Beatles," was in Grosvenor Ballroom in Lisgard. The Beatles had done a tour of Scotland and Allan (Williams) fixed this booking for them at the Grosvenor Ballroom for a promoter called Les Dodd in the summer of '60. The reason I was over there because it's on the other side of the river is because Gerry & the Pacemakers were appearing on the same bill. They had no connection apart from being another Merseyside group. Brian Epstein didn't come into the picture at all at that stage.

Alan Williams: I remember the occasion very well because I can remember the fee. It was ten pounds per group. Not ten pounds per person. It was ten pounds for Gerry & the Pacemakers and ten pounds for the Beatles.

Reading your book "The Man Who Gave The Beatles Away," can you recall taking The Beatles via minibus to Hamburg and the wonderful picture in front of the Arnhem monument with the great quote...

AW: "Their name liveth forever more." Arnhem was a cemetery that was a major military disaster in the last war where a lot of paratroops were shot out of the air. And it's a big war cemetery. It was a very emotional occasion because I can remember when we went to the cemetery 'cause I wanted to see it. Also I remember if you know the photograph that's in the book, you'll probably notice that Lennon was not in the photograph. He refused because even in those days he didn't want to know anything connected with war. He was a peace loving guy. Shortly afterwards, that peace loving guy, when we did a tour of the town of Arnhem, walked into a music shop and came out with a mouth organ that he never paid for. (laughs) But it was a very exciting trip because they drive on the wrong side of the road as we say in England and there were a lot of tram cars. We got stuck in the tram lines when this tram came roaring down and we couldn't get out of the tram tracks. That was almost a disaster. Finally when we did get to Hamburg late in the evening, we did actually hit a car.

George Harrison said that he felt The Beatles were never better than they were in Hamburg. Do you agree with that appraisal?

AW: Yeah, it was very sexy that their schooling was in Hamburg and when they came to the Cavern that's where they became polished and due to Bob's guidance 'cause Bob used to be known as "Dr. Rock." He used to give all the advice to the groups.

Bob, I understand that Brian Epstein relied on your advice regarding The Beatles very early on in their career.

BW: He came on the scene initially to dabble really because he hadn't in any way involved himself with groups prior to that. He relied upon Allan and I for advice on various matters. One of the things I told him was a question of fees. I was able to tell him first-hand through being the booker at the Cavern just what these Manchester groups got at the Cavern. So when the Beatles were booked to appear in Manchester, he obviously didn't want to undercut the price. To a large extent, he went along, he was indeed got by presentation and billing of the Beatles.

AW: Yes 'cause you see at that period in time, Bob and I were involved with a lot of groups. The Beatles were fairly newcomers. I mean Rory Storm and the Hurricanes and Gerry & the Pacemakers were all sort of Bob's groups that played in the Cavern. You see Brian Epstein was completely new to the business, totally new. He was a greenhorn so he had to rely. And we fortunately liked Brian Epstein, he was a gentleman. He wasn't a "Mr. Nasty" of show business which show business is riddled with. He really loved the Beatles. He was involved with them personally. Not just taking his percentage.

Allan, you were with The Beatles in Hamburg during their formative years. What was it like to walk down the 'Reeperbahn' in those days?

AW: It was very, very sort of garish, neon signs. In one building there'd be a club in the basement, a club in the ground floor. There'd be nude dancing. There'd be transvestite shows. It catered to every sort of perversion and every sort of pleasure. And it was 24-hours. I did it once. I started off at eight o'clock and I remember coming out of a club at 12 o'clock the next day. You totally lost track of time. It was a very exciting city.

Beryl Williams: (Allan's wife who was along for the trip): I remember the width of the streets and the lights, thousands and thousands of lights as being part of the atmosphere. I also remember the slight disappointment getting into the Indra Club. It was very disappointing going into the Indra. We thought this wasn't much better than Liverpool. After the spectacular sight of the Reeperbahn 'cause it wasn't in the Reeperbahn. I remember that.

AW: The Indra by the way was the first club that the Beatles played. And when we arrived they hadn't even bothered changing it into a rock and roll venue. There were still strippers there and the Beatles just couldn't believe it when we went into this plush carpeted place with strippers performing. (laughs) Because the other group were playing in the Kaiserkeller...Howie and the Seniors.

Allan, in your book about their 1960 Hamburg recording session with The Beatles and Ringo you speak about an acetate of a song called "Fever."

AW: Oh yes. This was the time that Rory Storm and the Beatles were playing at the same venue. I wanted to make a record with the singer called Wally out of Rory Storm's group. We found a recording studio. Ringo didn't play with the Beatles in those days but with Rory Storm. That's how they actually met. Wally wanted Ringo to play drums because he was used to him but he wanted the Beatles to back him and that's how that song came about.

Tell us the story behind your discovering the live Hamburg tapes and meeting with George and Ringo in the Seventies whereby George gave you sixteen uncut rubies for your wife Beryl's birthday.

AW: Funny thing about the rubies is that I put six of them in Sotheby's. You know Sotheby's has a Beatles auction every year and this was two years ago and I just got them back the other week because they didn't fetch their reserve, I think they fetched only 150 pounds. And it's taken two years to get them back so I'll stick them in another auction thing. The meeting was that I had the Hamburg tapes which was the Beatles live at the Star Club. I had them almost for ten years trying to sell them. Of course, the first natural thing to do and respectfully, I let the Beatles have first option which they said "no." They didn't like the quality of the sound and they didn't want to know them. So about four or five years later eventually they were released legitimately. The only thing that was not legitimate was that both Ted Taylor who owned the tapes and myself were completely ripped off. And they're still selling today. A chap called Paul Murphy who first released them with "Lingasong" copped for all the money and a guy called Halpern, I think he's dead now, a lawyer in New York. They copped for all the money.

Allan, in your book you print an interesting letter from Ringo Starr writing to the state of Texas requesting employment.

AW: Yeah, at one time he was with Rory Storm at the time and was considering emigrating to the States to become a cowboy.

Bob, is it true that you introduced Brian Epstein to The Beatles for the first time when he came to see them at The Cavern?

BW: The truth is, the books are totally wrong. I didn't know he was in the audience. He wasn't there in the Cavern audience as far as I was concerned you see. I went down to NEMS with them (to meet with Brian Epstein) because they asked me to go and it was a bit tricky that meeting because Brian was very hesitant. He didn't quite know how to put it to them (about offering to be their manager). Apart from that, he was wondering who I was, you see. So that particular meeting didn't quite amount to anything.

Didn't John introduce you as 'me Dad?'

BW: Yes. Brian looked around the room for the intros and

John came up with that quip.

Bob, discuss the Beatles transformation from leather toughs to a neat and clean image under Brian Epstein.

BW: It didn't happen overnight, they weren't transformed. It took him a while to persuade them to go along with this more civilized appearance. They wanted the informality that went with jeans and leather. There were various venues that they should have various suits on and they went along with this.

AW: Well can I ask you a question? Do you agree that he was right in putting them in suits?

BW: Well you've got to realize Allan, that this was what '62, '63. It isn't so much now with the advent of Dylan, and the hippies and heavy metal, anything went, you see. But in '62 and '63, there were various places where Brian wanted them to appear at. And the idea of them wearing that attire just didn't happen.

AW: Yeah, for a start, my own feeling is that they wouldn't have been accepted in the States at that time if they turned up in their leather gear, and their jeans and their scruffy appearance. You saw them as clean cut. Okay, they had these funny haircuts but I don't think you would have accepted them the way you did if they were scruffy.

John Lennon read your book and reportedly said it was the most accurate description of The Beatles career.

AW: In actual fact, I was over in the States last year and had a meeting with Yoko. She told me an interesting story that when he knew I was writing a book he got so angry that he actually shit himself because he knew the stories I could tell. When he was sent the galleys, the draft of the book, he was highly amused by it hence he wrote that lovely quotation that 'Allan Williams' book is the only book that gives the true insight on the Beatles.' Obviously he didn't remember certain places. Obviously I didn't. All these clever farts now who are writing books are pulling me up over certain dates like, "Oh, you didn't say that the channel crossing was New Haven." But, you know, if Bob and I tell these stories we're not interested in giving you the precise time and the flight number of the plane. We just tell the story.

What were your impressions of the fifth Beatle Stu Sutcliffe?

AW: Well Beryl can tell you the story of Stuart Sutcliffe arriving with his girlfriend Astrid when they were having a terrible time with Stuart Sutcliffe's mother. Can you remember that?

Beryl Williams: Yes, yes. In those days, young people still needed the privacy that they do now but it wasn't a done thing especially in the north where you brought a girl home to your mother's expecting to stay. There are still hangups about that now. You can do it elsewhere but definitely not at your mother's. They weren't used to that kind of relationship. They wanted to be close so they came to our house and Astrid was very grateful that she could escape. She wanted very desperately to make friends of Mrs. Sutcliffe and her daughters but she couldn't do it in the inhibited way that Mrs. Sutcliffe invited in her home.

What do you remember about Astrid, Beryl?

Beryl Williams: Extremely beautiful, and way ahead of her time I would think as far as her personal appearance was concerned. Very gentle and obviously very much in love with Stuart and they were an ideal pair. According to me, they were the greatest love story on this earth. Really. And I've always maintained that love story was one of the nicest things to come out of the Beatles affair.

We were curious to gauge your impressions of The Beatles, post-Cavern era.

BW: In August '61 in "Merseybeat." We had a pop music paper called "Merseybeat" which Bill Harry was the editor of. I wrote an article about the Beatles and this you've got to realize, it's so easy to be wise after the event. I came to certain conclusions in that article and I committed that article to black and white, to print. And what I said in that article about the Beatles just to give you one example. I started off the article by saying, "I don't think anything like them will ever happen again." So when they did the hit parade in this country and in your country in '64, that didn't surprise me one iota because two or three years before when nobody wanted to know about them I'd already said this.

AW: I don't think anybody could have visualized the world phenomenon that they became. They changed the entire youth way of thinking. We're going back twenty five years to when it was all happening. This is the reason why you're here. I'm sure you won't be here twenty years ahead talking about Boy George. Nobody could have visualized but at the same time you should have been here in the sixties. People say to us, aren't we sorry that we let them go. Just to be a part of that era, to be a cog in the wheels of the history of the Beatles is our reward. OK, we didn't go along for the gravy train. We didn't make a lot of money out of it but we were there and you can't take that away from us.

Bob, give us a sample introduction that you would have given The Beatles for one of their 294 performances there?

BW: We didn't have any curtains on the Cavern stage. And when the group went on-stage to tune up, they were quite evident to the audience which group it was. And I was mindful of this and therefore any long winded announcement was ridiculous. Everyone knew who was on-stage so I'd simply say "Here they are, it's The Beatles" and hopefully they'd go straight into a number. Continuity. At times they didn't, by the way, because I was very continuity conscious. You went straight into a number. I learned all this from Hollywood musicals by the way. The only time that the Beatles were ever filmed at the Cavern was by Granada Television. If you listen very carefully to that sequence when it's played from the beginning, you will hear a disembodied voice because I wasn't on-stage say "It's the Beatles." And I think it was "Some Other Guy" that they played. That's an indication that that's all one needed to say about them. Not a long preamble.

Please discuss some of your famous 'Woolerisms' like the one named after Brian Epstein, 'The Nemperor' and others.

BW: Yeah well Rory Storm was very much a showman in his presentation so I gave him the name "Mr. Showmanship." Faron from Faron and The Flamingos was "Mr. Fabulous." I once phoned Brian Epstein from "Merseybeat" office in Renshaw Street here in Liverpool and I knew it was him (on the phone) because I recognized his voice and because then you commuted to the city and they worked long hours. But they enjoyed it. They worked six and a half hours a night non-stop.

BW: I don't know where that Harrison quote comes from but I question the truth of that because it's nothing to do with them going around the theatres etcetera but they played the Cavern for two and a half years and I think at the Cavern, they were the Beatles, their natural selves.

AW: Yeah, I'd go along with that. Hamburg was a very artificial life. They were introduced to amphetamines because of the long hours. You must remember that Hamburg was a 24-hour city, non-stop. So when they'd finish work at maybe two o'clock in the morning, they'd start their entertainment. So it was really hard work.

BW: When you say that the Beatles worked long hours over there, they didn't at The Cavern. At the most, they'd work one hour. So they were able to pack into one hour everything. So obviously they were at their best for one hour whereas for six hours in Hamburg, they'd get jaded and faded.

AW: I would actually speak with him on the phone where you couldn't eventually. So it was all a play on Nems, and I said, "Is that "The Nemporer?" And he liked the idea. It appealed to him because of emperor. That's how that came about. And of course he was to use "Nemporer" for his telegraphic address on his note paper.

AW: So you can see the contribution that Bob and I made. When Brian took over the Beatles, they were already the hottest thing in Liverpool. All the spade work was done, all the hard work was done.

Finally do you feel that The Beatles would have stayed together longer had Brian Epstein not died?

AW: I'll answer that simply, no.

Beryl Williams: I don't think that they would have gone on because if you look back at any eighteen year old's career, whatever field they're in, they're very seldom with the same people earning a living at age twenty five for example. They seemed to have done everything and they all wanted to divert attention.

THE KINKS

RAY DAVIES OF THE KINKS LIVE AT THE TOWER THEATRE, PHILADELPHIA
PHOTO COURTESY: MICHAEL LESSNER

"You Really Got Me," "Lola," "'Til The End Of The Day," "Waterloo Sunset" and "Come Dancing" are among the brilliant rock tunes penned by The Kinks' lead vocalist and ace songwriter Ray Davies. Now celebrating more than three successful and colorful decades in the rock arena, The Kinks are one of the true touchstones of rock history. Ray Davies recalls the unforgettable night The Kinks shared a stage with The Beatles.

When did you first become aware of The Beatles?

I read an article about them before I heard them in the paper that said they were making totally British music and didn't use echo which interested me because my favorite group were the Ventures. And to me, the Beatles stole the Ventures rhythm sound and put their own things on top of it. And I saw them on television and I thought "Yeah, I could do this." You don't have to be pretty because I'm not mister good-looking. You don't have to look like Cliff Richard or Elvis Presley to be a pop singer. And I think what was good about The Beatles was that there was a sexuality, a hungry look, and an appealing look with girl fans, obviously. But they were not outwardly visually pretty to look at except Paul McCartney.

Didn't you play on the same bill with The Beatles?

We played a few times with The Beatles, three times. They opened for us once. (laughs) We turned up late because my brother was in prison in Denmark. We were doing a big concert in Denmark and we had to come back the following day to play at the N.M.E. Poll Winners concert. There was a riot at our show in Denmark and the police arrested Dave (Davies) and put him in prison. They let him out in time to get the last flight out of Denmark to do the concert. We got to the gig which is this big place at Wembley, London, this big concert hall. Our manager said "Quick, Quick, you're on after this act." And I said, "Who's on?" And I heard (imitates intro guitar line to "Ticket to Ride"). It was "Ticket to Ride" playing. And I said, "Well, that's the Beatles!" (laughs) And he said, "Well, you're on after them."

How about the other times you shared the stage with The Fab Four?

Before "You Really Got Me" was a hit, we did two shows where we went on just before them. What normally happened then was bands would come on and people would shout out "We want Ringo!," "We want Paul!." But with The Kinks, they listened, which was great, and also a sign that we had something. Oh, there was one show also where The Who, then called "The High Numbers," were on before us and then we were on just after them and The Beatles came on. It was quite a good package. We did two shows. The band got $100. The tickets were $2.

What were your impressions of The Beatles live?

I loved watching them. They were a good rhythm section. Ringo was a really good drummer. I think he was the best element in the live band at that time. He just played very well. The band knitted together very well, very nice sound.

THE FOUR SEASONS

L-R: FRANKIE VALLI, NICK MASSI, TOMMY DEVITO & BOB GAUDIO
COURTESY: RHINO RECORDS

rankie Valli and The Four Seasons reigned, along with The Beach Boys, as America's most popular band of the Sixties. With sales of more than one hundred million records and a well-deserved place in "The Rock and Roll Hall of Fame," Frankie Valli and The Four Seasons are a bona fide rock and roll institution. Frankie discusses his impressions of "The Fab Four" and recalls his brief meeting with his so-called "competition" in Italy, circa 1964.

When did you first discover The Beatles?

Well I had a reaction to the Beatles even before they came to America. The Four Seasons were in England in 1963. We were doing a tour there and the Beatles were in the audience watching the show. I picked up some records in England which were all those early Beatles songs that came out later on all the other different labels. I brought them back with me and we played them for Bob Crewe who was producing us at the time and of course I heard the songs in a totally different context. I told Bob Crewe that I heard these songs and I think they're great. I think we should record them. And he listened to them and loved them too but he said, "What we're going to do is write our own stuff. Everything will be tailor-made for the group." So I knew that the Beatles eventually were gonna bust through. I just liked what they were doing. They were doing it in such a way that it was unique, it was different. But there was also a lot of Everly Brothers in the early Beatles records.

You shared the same label Veejay Records with the Beatles for a short time and they put out an album called "The Beatles Vs. The Four Seasons—International Battle Of The Century" that is very rare today. What was your reaction to that album?

Oh, I thought it was neat. I really did think it was neat because we were both on Veejay Records and that record company came so close to exploding for some of the people they had on that label. They had Gladys Knight, and Jerry Butler and Betty Everett, and the Beatles, and the Four Seasons, and John Lee Hooker. And for some strange reason, the company had an awful lot of internal problems and they went bankrupt. But I thought it was a great idea. The album was only out for two or three months. There was a lawsuit. Fortunately, I happen to own two of those albums. They're worth a lot of money.

A lot of groups buckled under the pressure of The Beatles but The Four Seasons continued to thrive with many hit records.

It's really the old thing, you know. There were a lot of American groups who tried to change the style of what they were doing and become English groups. The Beach Boys, and the Four Seasons, and the Four Tops and the Temptations all stayed with doing what they did. And we weathered that whole storm. I mean there were other people having hits besides the Beatles. But a lot of American groups got lost under that. It's like waking up one day and you see a new guy on the block and you look in the mirror and say "I wanna look just like him" and you start trying to do things to yourself to look like him or sound like him. Everybody has to have their own identity. It's really very important and that's what we did. We said "Sink or swim we're going to stay with what we do" and it's the only chance that anybody could have. So we continued to enjoy success through the Beatles.

You've covered two Beatle songs in your career, "A Day In The Life" and "We Can Work It Out." Why did you choose to do those particular Beatles songs?

A good friend of mine was doing a soundtrack for a movie called "All Of This And World War II." His name was Lou Reisner. He also did some producing for Rod Stewart in the very early days and he came to us and told us he was doing this thing with the London Symphony Orchestra and he'd like us to do two cuts. We picked the sides we wanted to do and it all worked out very successfully.

Did you ever get a chance to meet The Beatles?

Yes, I did. The first time that I had an opportunity to spend any time with them was when I took a vacation after a long tour. I went to Italy. I pick up the newspaper there and find that the Beatles are appearing in Italy so I found out what hotel they were in and we went by the hotel and I spent about three hours just sitting around having a lot of fun. One of the people with me was a guy by the name of Charlie Colello who did a lot of the arrangements for us in the early days. He had a movie camera with him and the whole thing. We just took a lot of still shots and he used a lot of film. Went and brought it to somebody and had it developed and they told him that they lost it. (laughs) It was just a total waste. But we did spend time and we did realize that we liked each other. I never looked at anybody in this business as my competition. You do what you do and I do what I do and we can basically be doing the same thing. If anybody is buying a service from us, they're still uniquely different and their own way. So it wasn't as competitive. Today a lot of people in the business act like it's a little bit more competitive than it actually is. In the old days, there was more camaraderie between artists. Everybody was good friends. One artist might be listening to material to record and hear a song that might be right for someone else and call that person up and say, "I just found a song that's great for you." That doesn't happen too much anymore. Everybody is bent on being millionaires and living in L.A. with palm trees and all that.

JACKIE DeSHANNON

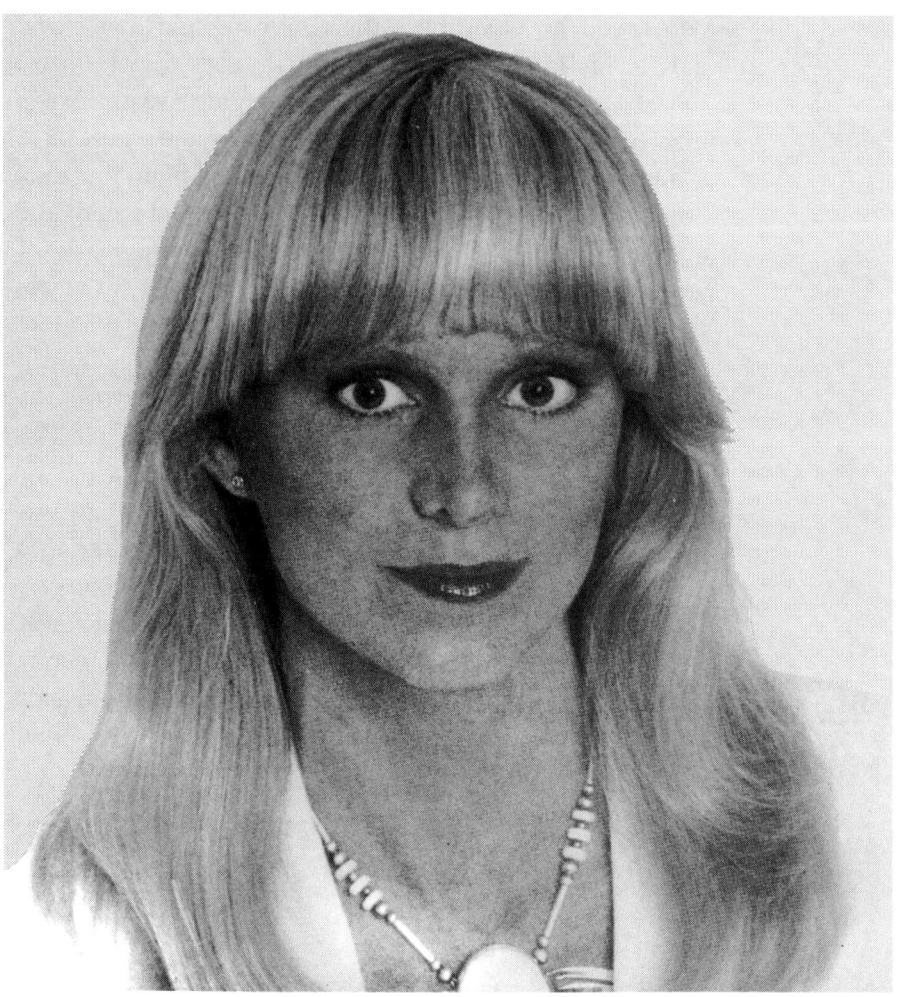

JACKIE DESHANNON PHOTO COURTESY: BOB CATO

Scoring such hits as "Put A Little Love In Your Heart" and "What The World Needs Now Is Love" and co-writing The Searchers' British Invasion gem "When You Walk In The Room," are among Jackie DeShannon's numerous achievements. A multi-faceted talent, Jackie could seemingly do it all. Back in 1964, Jackie was chosen by The Beatles as one of the opening acts on the band's first U.S. tour. Here Jackie shares her memorable experiences of hitting the road with John, Paul, George and Ringo.

What struck you about The Beatles?

Well, I think the sound that they had was really incredible. It was always such a big sound, very pure. There were so many groups playing in the local clubs and it was just a tremendous...the energy that I think somehow along the way we had lost for a period of time, they sent that back over our way. They reminded us what it was like in the beginning...really the energy.

There's a classic photo of you and George Harrison sitting on the floor playing Monopoly from the '64 tour. Do you remember that?

I've recently seen that! That was great! (laughing)

Weren't you a bit skeptical about The Beatles at first?

Well in the beginning I was a big Rolling Stones fan, still am. I liked the Beatles' later stuff. "I Want to Hold Your Hand," I really didn't know, I had my doubts. After the second or third single, I don't think anybody had a doubt of what was going to happen. But they always surprised us, luckily. (laughing)

How did you get picked to be one of the opening acts on The Beatles 1964 U.S. tour?

Well I think a lot of people wanted to do the tour. I was with a record company, Liberty, at the time and Brian Epstein, their manager, and the manager of our record company were very close and I had expressed a great desire to go on tour. And I was very lucky to be chosen.

Didn't Paul McCartney ease your stage fright before your first performance with The Beatles?

Right, that is true...at The Cow Palace (San Francisco). It's very true. I was very very nervous. And they all got out of their limos and came out and Paul came over and I was just sort of standing there. And I'll really never forget it. He was very very sweet and he said, "I've heard some of your music and it's really good and it's gonna be great so don't worry about it." He was really kind.

How did you go over with an audience made up of screaming Beatles fans?

Well no one went over well in the beginning. (laughs) It took a little while. I really adjusted my program. I did a lot of fast material. I did "Shout" and a number of things which were very uptempo. I ended up closing the first half from the other acts. They all had big records and it's very difficult when you're playing in front of 80,000 people who came to see the Beatles. They really were not interested in anything else. But I managed to do OK.

What was the Hollywood Bowl show like?

It was all great. We did six weeks of one-nighters, practically. And every night was better than the rest.

What were your impressions of the Beatles as a live unit?

Well you couldn't hear them very well, no. There was so much screaming. But it was always thrilling when you have a performer or performers that move an audience like that it's always very very exciting.

Any memories of hanging out with the group?

They were always very very nice. I think we really shared a lot...One of my most favorite times was in Florida where we were all sitting around singing the first songs that we could remember that we wrote. Some of the rhymes, you're hearing the Beatles now, but to hear an early song that maybe someone wrote at 14, it was amazing some of the rhymes you would come up with (laughs)...pie, and sky and so on and so forth. But they were very supportive and it was great, I have nothing but great things to say and very very nice happy memories.

You put out an album at the time called "Breaking It Up On The Beatles Tour."

Well I think unfortunately the record company sort of put it together to capitalize on the fact that I was touring with them at the time. I think it would have been nice if they'd done it and taken some time and put together a proper package. But I think some of the songs were not really records, some of them were indeed made as demos.

HARRY NILSSON

HARRY NILSSON & JOHN LENNON PLAYING POOL AT
THE RECORD PLANT, NEW YORK, NOVEMBER 1974.
COURTESY: BOB GRUEN/STAR FILE

a master tunesmith of the highest order, Harry Nilsson was a one-of-a kind rock and roll rogue. At a 1968 press conference for Apple Records, John Lennon and Paul McCartney announced to a startled press corps that Harry Nilsson was their favorite artist. A close friend of all four Beatles, Nilsson went on to work extensively with John Lennon, Ringo Starr and George Harrison. After John Lennon's tragic murder, Nilsson put his recording career on hold and became an avid proponent for gun control. Here the late, great Harry Nilsson regales us with his magical memories of the Fab Four.

What was your reaction when you first heard of John's death?

I reacted the way most people do when you lose someone

you like or love or care about. You go through a four stage period. First you get very angry, and you say "Dammit! Why him?" Then you get very very sad. Then you go through a period of acceptance and then the next stage is some sort of a resolve and either you Zen out on it and go "life is la la la" or you say 'I resolve to do something about it' and I chose the latter and got involved (being an anti-gun activist). I've never been an activist before but I'm enjoying it now because part of the reward is doing it because you know that it's right. We're gonna beat the NRA down.

There are a lot of crazy stories involving you and John, specifically regarding your drunken times in Los Angeles recording the "Pussycats" album and at "The Troubadour" club. Set us straight.

It started getting a little heavy with some of the guys, Bobby Keyes and Keith Moon, sorry Bobby, sorry Keith. John was the first one to say "Let's get straight here, whaddya say gang?" All of a sudden everything straightened out. He was straight as a die and he'd be there producing and doing a great job. It was pretty organized. It's just that the times that you do go out in public and, if you're with someone of the stature of Lennon, and you go to the Troubadour, somebody will make the biggest noise out of the smallest event. And that's what happened to us a couple of times. (in a crazy voice) You know you can't believe what you read in the papers, don't you?

What can we believe about the incident at "The Troubadour?"

Well I'll tell you what you can believe. He was wearing a Kotex on his head the week before but that was because he was perspiring a lot. We were thrown out of the Troubadour because a bunch of people, Peter Lawford, and Jack Haley, Jr., and some other people were going "Shhh! Shhh! Shhh!" 'Cause we were waiting for The Smothers Brothers to come on and we were singing "Can't Stand the Rain," you know that song, Ann Peebles? And we got the place singing a little bit and we had a nice time waiting for Tommy and Dicky and people were making more noises with their "Shhh's." And all of a sudden eight gargantuans came over and threw us out. That happens to a lot of people.

Tell us about the time you appeared live with John Lennon in Central Park.

I went on-stage with John in front of about 200,000 kids in Central Park. It was for the crippled kids. It's an amazing feeling of power and influence you have because at one point you're looking out at this sea of faces, you don't know that you're the object of their eyeballing. In that park, I remember looking at them and saying, Wow, if John at that moment had said, (imitates Lennon's voice) "See that guy in the 47th row, I don't like him!" They would have eaten him! (laughs)

What are your recollections of recording "Pussycats," the album John produced.

We flew people in from all over the world. We stayed together at a beach house for a month and a half. We had fleets of limousines organized to go up to Warner Brothers every night. We spent four to five months just working on it. John and I spent the last month just working on it ourselves with the engineer. We took it very seriously. Listen to the values on it, it's very good. In fact, I haven't heard it in years but I listened to it recently and said, "Hey, that's good!" "Many Rivers To Cross," dynamite! "Old Dirt Road," not bad.

What's the story about the cremated remains of Mal Evans, The Beatles' longtime roadie, being lost in the mail?

He was killed by a handgun by the police in one of those incidents. I got this phone call, went down to the jail where they were keeping his girlfriend as a material witness or something, asking her questions. I got her out and then they said, "What do you want done with the body?" And his folks lived in England someplace, I didn't know how to reach them, so I said "Well, burn it." So they got the ashes and they have these different kinds of boxes...cardboard boxes, tin boxes, brass boxes and gold boxes with diamonds. I said, "So how are you going to send him back to England?" And they said, "Well, we've got this nice little paper bag here. " And I said, "No, no, no, that's nice. I'll go for the brass, it's not too ostentatious." At the time, there was this rash of ghoulery. There were these professional modern day ghouls who used to steal these...it says remains of the deceased or something, and if they feel a heavy one, they know it's either brass, gold or lead. And they used to steal them. So what happened was that I mailed him to his parents and I get a call a week later from Neil Aspinall at Apple who says, "Harry, where's Mal?" I said, "I sent him, Neil. He's in the mail." So he says, "C'mon man. They're starting to give me some pressure from over here." So I said, "Look, I'll put a tracer on him." So I called Forest Lawn. "Where's my friend?" And they said, (in horror voice) "Well, we've had these ghouls running around. " And I said, "You've got to be kidding! You mean you've lost my friend?" It turns out that he did turn up and you'll never guess where...the dead letter office. (laughs) I swear to you. It sounds bizarre but that's what happened. Eventually we sent it on to his folks who, by the way, before spilling his ashes in the ground near the Thames, the wind came up and blew them into the water so now he's lost in the Thames someplace up there saying hello to Keith (Moon) and John.

YOKO ONO PHOTO COURTESY: FRANCESCO SCAVULLO

YOKO ONO

Vilified by Beatle fans for over two decades as the real reason the group ultimately split, Yoko Ono carries on in her time-honored fashion of quiet dignity. John and Yoko were one of the most famous couples of all time, the love they felt for each other transcended all things material. From "Oh Yoko" to "Dear Yoko," John's love songs written for his wife reflect the depth of their love and commitment to each other. An accomplished avant-garde artist, poet and musician, Yoko Ono is a consummate survivor. Here in two separate conversations, Yoko shares her poignant memories of John.

What are your thoughts on John Lennon receiving a star on The Hollywood Walk Of Fame?

It's an incredible honor and I'm very happy that a lot of people worked for it and I'm very thankful. I remember John and I walking in Hollywood and John was looking at the stars and saying, "Well, what do you think about me?." (laughs) I remember that so, yes, it took a long time but still there are many many years to come that we can enjoy and I'm very thankful.

Do you feel a lot of the positive aspects happening with John now, the "Imagine" film, the star, will counteract a lot of the negativity as well?

Let's not talk the book, let's not talk about the book! (laughs) Yes, I think you're right about that. We didn't plan it that way but it's really a blessing.

Is "Woman" your favorite John Lennon song and what did you think of the "Imagine" film?

Yes, I love the song "Woman" naturally but it's very hard to say if that's the song that I love the most. I love all John's songs. When I saw the film, I was totally emotional. It impressed me very much. I was not critical at all. It was just a fantastic experience for me.

Was there anything about it that made you uncomfortable?

Well yes it did get a total endorsement from me. The result I thought was better than I expected. It's a brilliant film and I'm very thankful to both of these gentlemen (Andrew Solt and David Wolper) for making such an incredible film.

You're an experienced filmmaker yourself. Why did you let someone else do the film?

Well a lot of things we had to learn after John's death and all of us had to grow up. Many fans, initially, told me that I should take over the project. I should make sure that it's going to be alright, etcetera. The fans and myself, all of us, had to learn together that that's not the way to go. We had to think about seeing a film made that is very objective and had a good balance of what it really was about. And so I feel that I gave up my power to give power to the film.

When you received word that John would be receiving a star on Hollywood Boulevard, what was your reaction?

It was a very emotional moment as I've said before. It flashed in my mind immediately of the time that John and I walked in Hollywood. And John was pointing out, reading all the names, and wondering why he wasn't there.

How does it make you feel?

To me, it means that there's so many beautiful people still in the world who wished well for John and who still love John and made this happen and I'm very thankful to them. And also in the future, for many many years to come that this particular star will be enjoyed by so many people in the world and they will come to see it here and they will get the benefit of it.

Does the film set the record straight whereas "The Ballad Of John And Yoko" may have been inaccurate?

I don't think that "The Ballad of John and Yoko," the TV film, had any inaccuracy in that sense and I thought that that was a good film as well but that was of course a docudrama which is not a documentary and therefore it was fiction in a way in that sense. And of course this film is a totally different thing in the sense that the two films as almost the media was totally different.

Why weren't the other three Beatles interviewed for the film and have they seen it? If so, what was their reaction?

JOHN LENNON IN PHILADELPHIA, 1974
PHOTO COURTESY: MICHAEL LESSNER

I think that the film has such an incredible impact that it doesn't need to have anything added to it, nothing should be taken out of it. It's a completely beautiful film on its own and that's how I feel about it.

What prompted you to document your life on film?

Both John and I were filmmakers. John started to make films as well when we met. We made many films actually and some of the footage came from that. And also some footage were just from home movies and I'm sure that in this day and age all of you have an experience of going to Jamaica and taking a long family film and coming home and showing it to your friends. And we were just family and we did that.

Should this film have been made five years ago or is now the right time?

Well the timing is really something that's up to them, it's like a blessing. I didn't time it this way. But also yes it's true, it was too difficult for me to even consider making a film or asking someone to make a film, that's how it was.

Where does "Real Love," the beautiful unreleased song that appears in the film, come from?

That comes from the so-called 'Dakota Days.' (laughs) It was a song that was supposed to be part of a musical that John and I were intending to make. And it may still become one.

Was it difficult for you to watch the film on an emotional level?

Well I tried to lock my emotion to see the film, and see it from an objective point of view but obviously it was very painful for me but at the same time extremely sweet. It was a bittersweet feeling watching the film.

Has Sean seen the film?

Sean was sitting next to me when we saw the film. He was very intent and afterwards he said, "It's a very good film, mama." But at one point when they showed the 'Two Virgins' record cover, I as a mother was a little bit concerned about how he felt so I looked at him and he just said, "That's very important, that's an historical important document" and I was saying, "Oh, I see" and I don't know about the Eighties' kids. So, alright, that's how he feels about it (laughs) and it's alright, I thought.

Watching the film, did you feel removed from it, like it all happened a long time ago?

We always shared that generation didn't we? And it's such a nostalgic feeling seeing it and it could be yesterday and it could be a hundred years ago, that's how I feel about it.

Will the film surprise people?

I don't think that it's going to surprise people. The old fans are going to think, "Oh, it's John, isn't it." And it is John He was a very complex person and all facets of his emotion and his life have really been covered. And you will see it from all different angles what John Lennon was all about.

John receiving his Star was a long time coming with many petitions and also the movie happening now all seems like perfect timing.

Well, as far as I'm concerned, this particular project was going on since last year. People getting in touch with me and saying how about this, and writing letters and that was going on parallel to many of things that were going on like "Lost Lennon Tapes" or this documentary film and to me, it seems like another marvelous coincidence that it's happening now.

Does it worry you being outside at an event like the star celebration with so many people around?

You can't just always be hiding in a box, you know. I'm used to being out and about and I think that basically most people wish well for this event and it's a celebration so I'm not particularly worried about it.

John gave back his M.B.E. (Member Of The British Empire). Do you feel if he was still here today he would have given back the Star?

No. John would have loved it. L.A. is a very special city for him. We had very beautiful times here together actually when I think about it. We had two anniversaries here too. He went to primal therapy here and this is where he met Elvis. Of course, everybody knows about his love for New York City. He liked the sky line, the palm trees, the beautiful sky that's always blue. It was a very special moment whenever we came here so I'm sure that he would have thought this a great honor. As I said before, he was always wondering why he wasn't there.

In the film, John talks about his problem with drugs saying it was not good to tell people to say no to drugs as people would rebel against it.

Well he was never proud of taking drugs but also he didn't want to be a hypocrite. He owned up the fact that he took it. But also he wanted to warn the young generation not to take it. He was a father too, you know.

How did he kick his drug habit?

Well, he had an incredibly strong will and he just did it.

Do you have any plans to write your book in the wake of the slew of Lennon books that have been published?

Well a lot of people are saying that. I think about that too. But I don't want to do it when I'm going to be writing out of a defensive feeling. So I just have to wait until I can just write it the way I want to write without thinking about other books. In the future, it's a possibility.

How does it feel knowing that John was selected by the people to receive the Star?

It's extra special that the people pushed to let it happen. That's a very important point. By the way it might help the film. But I do know in all fairness that they weren't trying to control the situation or anything at all. It's a totally separate thing. And as you know, he was a "Working Class Hero" and part of the people, and he's got the power from the people back, which is very very special for me.

What are your thoughts about John being exposed to the younger generation with his film?

Well it's a historical document as well as a document of John's life and it's to do with the Sixties and our generation and all of us having had to go through a lot of experiments, some beautiful ones and some not so beautiful ones. And I think they've all heard about the bed-in and things like that so it's good to see it in the documentary.

It must have been an extremely moving experience to compile "Onobox?"

Yes, it was quite a trip. It was like opening Pandora's box. (laughs) But it was exciting as well because there's songs I've found where I went "Oh, I'd forgotten about this!" So there's some new ones in there, meaning new old ones that were never out there before.

Why didn't "Mrs. Lennon" make it?

Everybody says that, it's amazing. And I wanted that one in there too but for some reason I couldn't get it in. Why? Because of "London Jam." I wanted to keep that kind of music quality and it was a totally different direction so you just can't put "Mrs. Lennon" in the middle of that stuff.

Any plans to re-release your Apple solo records?

I suppose it depends on how well the box set does. Initially I had in mind a nine CD set. The other one would have been "Mrs. Lennon," "Have You Seen The Wind?," "John and Yoko Wedding Album" and a little bit of "Two Virgins" in there too. The other one would have been political, a "Sometime in New York City" thing. And also the third one would have been live so there was enough for nine really but they said six and I think it was a good decision because this way it's very tight.

For the past ten years you've devoted yourself to preserving John's memory. It seems like this is the first time you've actually been able to do your own project. That must be very gratifying.

It's true. I mean I'm just very thankful that this happened. It's like being given a second life. I'm very surprised that anyone was interested in doing this.

What would John have thought about "Onobox?" Would he have felt some better Yoko Ono songs were omitted?

Oh sure. Definitely. I think that he would have liked more of the "Don't Worry Kyoko," that kind of heavy stuff in it.

There was a great quote of yours where you said "We ruined each others careers."

(Laughs)

In a way it's true. But you did push each other in different directions.

I know. Because we were both artists and the first concern of all artists would be that the creative juices and inspiration could flow. So that's what we had really. We met each other and somehow we went "Wow!" Not just as men and women, but as artists and we felt that we were really discovering new grounds in music. That was much more exciting than protecting our careers.

Is it true that you felt relaxed enough to experiment with your own ideas because of John's simplistic musical style?

I felt very relaxed with the kind of contemporary classical kind of music I was in and then with the avant-garde and all that. You get into a head trip and you just kind of lose the quality of being close to your body. It gets more and more removed from your body with the headtrip. Going back to your body in that with a rock beat and everything was great and relaxing. And for John he had this daring, daring side of him and I think he was repressing that a little with the success of the Beatles and all that thing. Here he had a chance of just doing what he wanted. (laughs) Which was going with a guitar like crazy which he did.

That brings up our next question. John's guitar playing on your songs was very different from his guitar work with The Beatles.

Especially with "Why" for instance. You hear his guitar playing and you think "Where did that come from?" Well of course it came from him. (laughs) It's just an amazing trip he was going through with that one.

Your music also had that effect on other people who played on your records like Ringo Starr, George Harrison and Eric Clapton.

We didn't talk much but we understood each other on a musical level. I think that most musicians had fun with my music because they could just relax and be themselves and try something new. So musicians usually understood my work and liked it.

We've read nothing but glowing reviews of "Onobox." How does that feel to be finally on the receiving end of good news?

Well I still don't know. It's hard to feel that yet. I'm totally surprised with the initial reception. I think part of me was thinking I was going to get the same kind of treatment I got when these things initially came out, which was like twenty five years ago. (laughs) Then they were incredibly objectionable shall we say. So then suddenly this initial flood of reviews which seem to show they kind of understand what I was doing then. I'm just totally surprised. I can't get over it.

JOHN LENNON IN PHILADELPHIA, 1974
PHOTO COURTESY: MICHAEL LESSNER

Your philosophy "I love you and up yours" really typifies you. It's nice that you can finally say that to people.

If it was just "I love you" I would have killed myself. But it was this "Up yours" quality which kept me going.

John was in Bermuda in 1980 and he heard The B-52's and some other new wave groups in a disco and got really excited, calling you up saying "They're doing you." When you finally heard the music of The B-52's and Nina Hagen, who were greatly influenced by you, how did that make you feel?

I was totally amazed but also it was not just amazement. I was just very thankful that they would be saying things outright that there was some factor that I inspired them. Since Yoko and the Plastic Ono Band and even with "Have You Seen The Words In The Wind" and "Mrs. Lennon," there's a certain trick that I'm doing with my voice. It's going against the grain of the so-called commercial singing. So that kind of fraility that you leave it alone rather than smoothing it out with echoes. Even in the initial stage, John would sort of immediately notice something on the radio and go "Listen to that. They got our stuff." We kept saying that really but we didn't know about the B-52's. And then we found out that they sort of have given me credit and I think John enjoyed that. We were very thankful.

Have you ever considered working with The B-52's?

They're doing well on their own. (laughs)

It would be an interesting pairing.

Maybe. (laughs)

We read a review of "Double Fantasy" that came out in England before John's passing and they praised your work and panned John which is ironic.

In "Double Fantasy" what John was trying to do was really communicate the idea of men and women dialogue. And for that he was not really trying to musically top anybody. I think he was really trying to make music that would communicate a message. He was doing it in a very relaxed manner which I thought was very good. I think that was very good. What he communicated was a very very courageous thing to do and on top of it, if the music was difficult or so called avant-garde or too gutsy, I don't think he would have communicated. All that he took as a guy with that dialogue was trying to show that the guys do have vulnerabilities as well and the music went with that.

Has the acceptance of "Onobox" inspired you to do a new studio album?

I'm already starting a project and I'm in the process of recording some stuff which may not become a record. It's another kind of experiment in a new area I've never done anything in so that...we'll see where it goes.

Let's go back to 1960 and your first encounters with the avant-garde and John Cage. What was your initial response?

After my college years I came down to New York and I met

a few sort of interesting composers like Edgar Varez and John Cage. All the others that I met were fine composers and everything but John Cage sort of stood out even amongst them for being so left field and interesting. That was like in the end of the Fifties. What John Cage's music did for me is to sort of reassure me that it's alright to do what you believe in and go that route.

It seems during that time in New York there was an amazing exchange of ideas. Do you feel that freedom of ideas helped spawn the avant-garde movement?

It wasn't cutthroat or anything like that but each one of us were definitely very different and very independent. If I said I felt Cage's way was it and I went with it, some Cage people might say your music has nothing to do with Cage (laughs). And it's true. In a way each one of those people that were in that group in the early days I'm sure they feel that they had a unique thing. But it was a very exciting time because they were all original and unique and were doing something that was really before their time.

Tell us about your musical background. We understand your father discouraged your involvement with music.

I think that the environment I was in was a heavily intellectual kind of environment and my father was into three B's meaning Bach, Brahms and Beethoven. I keep saying that but at the same time he was the one who turned me onto people like Alvin Berg which is like turning me on to very very contemporary music. So it wasn't just the three B's but basically he believed in that. It was all in the classical field. Also I think understandably in those days that he just had this concept that women are not made to be composers because just looking around and just seeing that there was no female name in the field of composition. It never occurred to men in that generation that maybe that was because of prejudice or whatever. (laughs) He just sort of simply thought that would not have been a very easy direction for me to go into.

Being a performance artist, author, amongst other things, how do you think your endeavors have helped shape you as a songwriter? Did it provide a different artistic scope and approach?

I think that I was writing songs before I put out the book

"Grapefruit" and I was writing poetry separately. The kind of poetry that I was writing was kind of like e.e. cummings. That was probably because I thought that was cool. It doesn't necessarily mean that was my innate form. It's just that I was always interested in writing poems and I was always interested in writing music. The natural thing for me to do was write songs I suppose.

Listening to your songs again on "Onobox," have any of your compositions taken on new meaning?

I don't know. I didn't look at it that way. I was just listening from a point of view as to whether I should drop some songs because I didn't have enough space. But then again there's some songs that are musically not up to par because of the remix so I remixed them. In terms of whether the songs changed in my mind, it just seems I was more feeling a kind of pain opening the Pandora's Box and my memory about the days when I wrote those songs. Because I was in a position where people were attacking me and not appreciating my music, I was like in the underground in a way but at the same time in a very strange way famous. As John said, "The most famous unknown women." So I was an unknown person and an unknown writer so there was a certain fierceness in my belief of my own work because otherwise you couldn't survive without it. You're not getting any support from the world so you have to support yourself. (laughs) So I kept on believing in those songs and I still do.

Did a healthy competition exist between you and John where you pushed each other towards excellence?

There was definitely a good healthy thing going. I didn't notice so much in terms of he writes a song so I write one. Not that kind of thing. I think both of us had an incredible blessing in a sense regardless of what's going around in our environment. Say in John's case what's going around in his environment, he's got this thing that sort of the words and the music came through him. It was just there. So that was that. In my case too. It wasn't so much that somebody was creating or not creating, it just came through whenever. And sometimes it doesn't come through and then sometimes it came through and it was uncontrollable in a way. The fierce competitive dialogue that we had was when we were actually making music in a situation like "Why." It was almost not like a dialogue. It was like topping each other, like a music bite. The intensity of "Why" comes from that we were really gung-ho about topping each other. (laughs)

A lot of people may be surprised but when you met John you really didn't know much about The Beatles.

Well I think now you listen to what I was doing and then you would understand that it's nowhere near the Beatles. (laughs) It was very different.

When did you realize the significance of The Beatles?

Well because I was sitting in the sessions all the time with John that it started to hit me that "This is good." But basically the music is so pleasant as well. So you're sitting there and thinking that's a good thing. It really relaxed me as a writer and started to open up a whole area of writing and I just felt good about it. So I don't regret any of that. But yes career wise, I might have ruined my career, but I gained a lot in return.

You actually sang background vocals on several Beatle records including "Birthday" and "The Continuing Story Of The Bungalow Bill." Was that fun?

Hmmm..fun is not the word for it. (laughs) Nervous, maybe. It was alright.

"Onobox" is broken up into six CD's with specific titles. Tell me what comes to mind with each starting off with London Jam."

I'm amazed with the reception that it's getting now and I still can't get over it.

"New York Rock".

I love it. It's great, great stuff I think. It's very me. That one is one that I feel comfortable with, that era.

"Run, Run, Run."

It has to do with communicating that message of women's plight. During the time of the recording of the whole thing I was very aware while I was recording it.

How about "Kiss Kiss Kiss."

That's a CD to me at this point that is very painful to think about.

"No No No."

That too is kind of painful. It's very interesting that "London Jam" and "New York Rock" really don't hit me as painful CD's. But "Kiss Kiss Kiss" and "No No No" are both sort of painful stuff for me.

Tell me about your unreleased solo LP "The Story" which is included on your "Onobox".

Well I just chucked it, you know. (laughs). I shelved it. I thought that it would never come out again. The reason is that John and I got back together. It was a very important time for us. I knew how the world was for me and about my work and if I put it out then the critics would have been kind of mean on a personal level. Musically I like it.

"O'Oh" sounds so contemporary that we at first thought it was a new cut.

I didn't even find the track myself. I think it was found by Rob Stevens who did the remix with me and all that. While we were sequencing he found all these tracks. One was "Pot Belly" and one was "O'oh." We were saying that "O'oh" sounds really contemporary. I remember that song but I was not gonna put it out because at the time when I put together that song the musicians were very sort of professional musicians and were sort of sniggering about it because it was too soft. I didn't have the energy to push them and go through it in a way. Vocal-wise there was only a rehearsal vocal on it. Rob Stevens said it was really a contemporary song and I wouldn't have thought about putting it on. When I heard it I thought that it was good. So I put a new vocal on.

Looking through the liner credits we were amazed by the stellar musicians who played on the record. People like Ornette

Coleman and Mick Jagger. How did Mick Jagger wind up playing guitar on "Winter Is Here To Stay?"

Well it's because he came to our session and was fooling around with John and we were starting to jam. And John just went, "Yoko, go ahead." So I did it.

What do you feel you learned from John on an artistic level and what did you add to his art?

My feeling is that you have to figure it out because both John and I were just doing what we can do. I'm not objective about it so I can't say what influence I gave John, I wouldn't know. And something that you have to ask John and John is not around. For me the biggest thing that happened was that I discovered the rock beat from him and also the fact that he had this incredible daringness and, of course, I had a little myself. But it's like that was really great, that was reassuring so together I suppose we became more daring and therefore the world couldn't take us. (laughs)

One heavily political album you did with John in 1972 was "Sometime In New York City" which would probably be well suited for today's political market. What do you recall about making that underated album?

We were at the Bank Street apartment. We were still naive at that point thinking that if we do that together it would probably communicate. It was like the Berchtold Brecht style. Now in hindsight when I think about it, each period, Bank Street period or Ascot period, on a personal level we were very happy. And also we were very lucky that we had each other. Especially for me, I was very lucky that I had someone who had such belief in my work. Just one man but that helped. I'm not made of iron so like most people believe that I am made of iron (laughs) and that I could stand anything and could survive anything myself. But the fact that really helped me was that John was around. Even in the jokes that I make in my songs John would laugh. So I would think if it's funny to him then it was okay.

Most people perceive you as being hard and serious but listening to your music and talking with you, it seems you have quite a sense of humor. It was kind of like George Harrison being the "Quiet" Beatle when in fact he could be as zany as the others.

Oh, George has a sense of humor. Well of course Ringo is well-known for his sense of humor. I think that just the fact that I jump from one media to the other within the musical homes, like I don't stick to blues, I don't stick to heavy rock, I don't stick to pop. Even in one album. There's a certain kooky side of me and that's me. I can't be any other way. And John used to laugh about that. John used to have fun about it. (laughs)

One of your most joyous collaborations with John was "Happy Xmas (War Is Over)" which receives its fair share of airplay each holiday season.

We made it over breakfast. It was great but then we had a kind of argument right after it and then we totally had forgotten about it. It was so funny because when we made the song it was great, we were together and we were feeling this sort of peace and love and the next moment we were arguing. When we remembered it it was too late for Christmas. (laughs) But we were saying "Let's push it out, let's push it out" and we pushed it out but it was too late. So when we made it John was saying "Let's top 'White Christmas' with this." But the way we did it was all wrong, like putting it out after Christmas. (laughs)

You worked with Lenny Kravitz on a new version of "Give Peace A Chance." Do you feel that there's a reawakening of that kind of late Sixties social and political consciousness happening today spawned by you and John?

I think so. What happened was after "Starpeace" there was a time when I just got tired of it. Last year I was saying to Sean, because he started to get so political, I was just saying, "Sean, just relax about it because your Dad and Mom did a lot. We did it because we wanted you to have a happy life and not sort of painful kind of life like we had so please relax about it. We did a lot but the world didn't change and it probably wouldn't change, so don't try it." And that was a really conservative remark but anyway that's how I felt. When I think about my child, I start getting conservative and worry that maybe he would go through the same kind of tumultuous lives that we went through. So then you know what he said? He wasn't sort of perturbed at all. He said, "Well Mommy, I don't think so. I don't agree with you. I think the Nineties are gonna be great. It's gonna be fine. We have to make it happen." (laughs) So I said that I was sorry that I said anything because I suddenly realized he's not gonna be influenced by that kind of negative talk. It was really amazing when he said it was up to us to have to make it happen. "Oh, alright." Don't I know that? (laughs) But suddenly it was like Sean waking me up again. It's understandable that I get sort of down sometimes. We all do. But basically I think that this is the only way. We have to do it inch-by-inch.

You recently did your first performance piece for quite some time. Do you plan on doing more in the future?

No, that was just because Shellut Moon Moon was one of my closest friends from way back and it was a tribute to her so I felt I should do a performance piece and I so did. Some people say "London Jam" is great now and you should go back and do that again. But I did it then. I don't have to repeat myself.

What do you recall about The Plastic One Band's premiere performance in Toronto which is documented on the "Live Peace in Toronto" LP?

We bumped into Little Richard in the hall and said hello. Then we were ushered in some room and we were just nervously waiting for our turn. Did you know that the Doors were supposed to go after us and they decided not to? (laughs) It was a let down for us because we would have enjoyed their performance. It was great. I know that later we found out that not everybody was excited by the fact that I was up on the stage with John. When I was up there I didn't really feel that way. There's a certain feeling that there's some people who are looking not particularly happy and antagonistic towards me but you forget those things when you're up there.

Will that show ever be issued on CD?

I don't know.

Since the "Lost Lennon Tapes" has ended, are there plans for a box set of unreleased material?

Yes. Elliot Mintz is doing it. He did the show and he knows all the ins and outs. He's compiling it now for a CD box. Hopefully it'll come out this autumn.

We'd like some thumbnail sketches of a few of your songs starting with "Approximately Infinite Universe."

That was like a story of my life. I was not the woman in Sappora. I'd never been in Sapporo at the time. (laughs) I only visited Sapporo after 1980. So it was just that feeling, that's me. I can say that this whole "Onobox" is like a woman's diary. It's like my emotional journey.

"Walking on Thin Ice" was a big hit for you.

"Walking On Thin Ice," yes, that was also me I suppose. At the time I was not realizing how closely it was me.

There's early versions of "I'm Losing You" and "I'm Moving On" from "Double Fantasy" with Rick Nielsen and Bun E. Carlos from Cheap Trick playing on them. Why didn't they make the final cut for the album?

Well because I think that John decided on the other versions we made afterwards to be on "Double Fantasy" and all that. They're great tracks so there might be a reason to come out. I think there was a lot of a contractual legal situation and I'm not going to deal with it.

There's been some talk that you're considering writing your autobiography. Where does that stand?

I think this box is the closest to an autobiography. Being an artist I think this may be the only way this story can be told.

I have to think about that. Maybe there will be one in the future. Never is a strong word and I wouldn't say never.

If a listener knew all your songs backwards and forwards would they have a pretty good idea of who are as a person?

I wouldn't know. I think that you can know a lot about me. It's not a situation where I'm writing a song in a very controlled way like some people do. Like let's make this into a hit song or whatever. It's like something that came through me and from me through my life. It's really my blood, sweat and tears, that kind of thing. I'm sure there's a lot of me in there that you can sort of look into.

Around the release of "Double Fantasy" John spoke of the possibility of a Yoko Ono solo LP coming out called "Yoko Only." Was that really in the plans?

I think that John was always telling me that I've got to do it just to show them. But there was no sort of very planned thing at the time.

Sadly in December 1991, John's beloved Aunt Mimi passed away. How do you remember her?

I mean I lost a friend in a way because we became good friends, especially after John's death, two women crying away. We exchanged a lot of reminiscences about John. So she was there for me and now she's not. But for her it was very difficult after John's death. She was feeling that life was too overbearing because he was not around.

Were they still close with Mimi living in England and John in America?

Not necessarily. Depending on the year. Some years they were close, some years they weren't. But she felt like John was her only world. She was very much into John. So after John's death she felt like her world was shattered. So it was very hard for her to live every year, surviving like that. So in a way maybe it's a blessing for her. It was amazing she survived over ten years after John's death. But of course it's interesting, John was always saying that Mimi's gonna survive me.

Spy magazine got hold of a tape which is purportedly a John Lennon audio diary from 1979 and printed a transcript of the contents. Was John keeping an audio diary?

> No, I don't know where they got that from. I'm not aware of it. I heard about it and I thought that it just probably was an outtake of the "Playboy" interview. There was no audio diary. There is a private cassette tape of Sean and John talking. Maybe they got hold of it. You know how those bootleg people get hold of things in an amazing way. (laughs) Maybe that's what happened.

If you had to place one John Lennon and one Yoko Ono song in a time capsule, what songs would you choose?

> When you said time capsule, the first word that came to me was "Imagine." (laughs) That's one. For mine...blank. I don't know. Who knows?...In fact, "Imagine" would be fine for both of us.

JULIAN LENNON

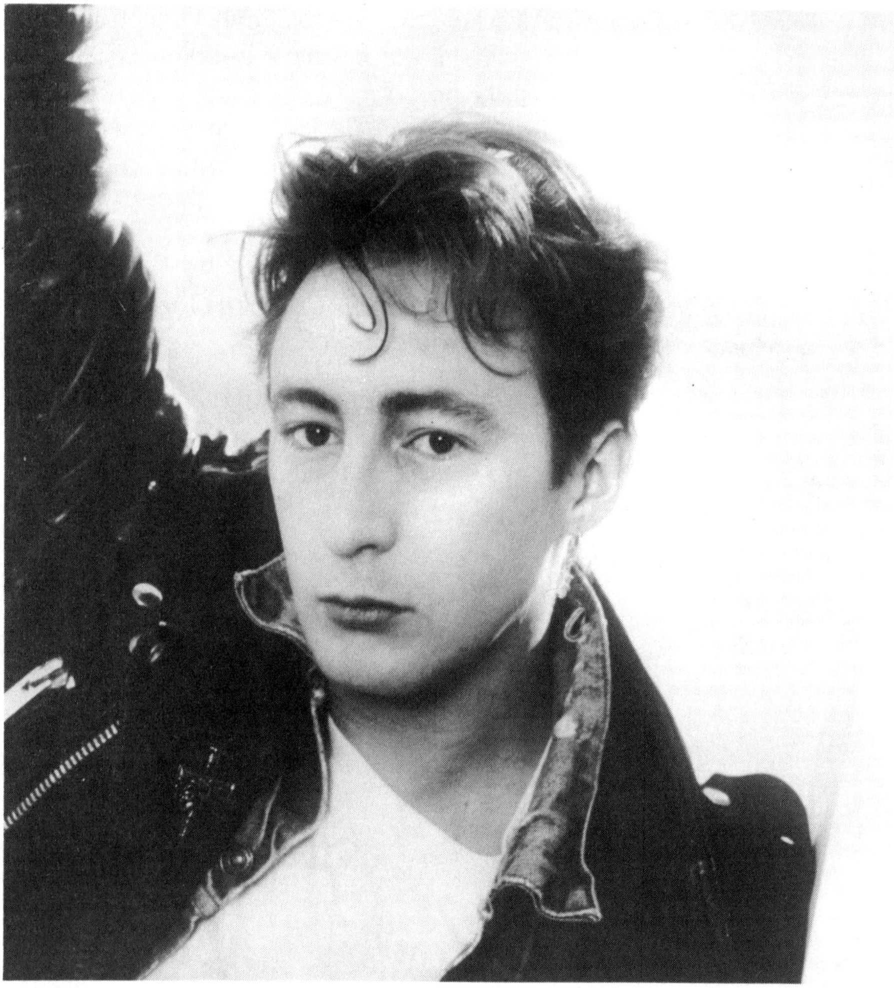

JULIAN LENNON **PHOTO COURTESY: ATLANTIC RECORDS**

When you're John Lennon's son and you're attempting to carve out your own musical career, you're setting yourself up for a serious critical bashing. After achieving major success with his debut LP "Valotte," the musical tables have turned on Julian and he's had a difficult time of late setting the charts on fire. Despite his lack of recent commercial success, Julian's continued to evolve as a recording artist, no longer a shadow of his father but a distinctive and promising talent in his own right.

Why do you feel you've gone from having immense popularity to relatively minor success?

I think it was the critics that lead people astray in that sense. I think generally the majority of the listeners out there were relatively into me and it's only when the critics came along and started saying certain things about comparisons, and making unconstructive criticism that people started going "Oh well, maybe he is this or that way." Because of all of that I sort of denied myself of who I am, my influences and everything else. It was the first time really with this album ("Help Yourself") that I said, "Screw that!" I've been around a little bit now. I didn't disappear. I've still been struggling working. There's things that I've had to resolve and figure out but seven, eight years on I'm still around and I don't see myself disappearing.

With its distinctive "Strawberry Fields" quality, tell us how "Saltwater" came about.

The majority of the music was written prior to me getting involved. This was actually the turning point for me that this was very Beatlesque, what am I going to do? The one main thing that I wanted to contribute to that was the original sounds. So I went on a hunt to find the original mellotron, string and flute sound from the past. There were things I like about it a lot but obviously I was a little nervous at first. And my producer Bob Ezrin said to me, "Jules, don't deny yourself this, it's part of you. Go for it!" And I redemoed it using the original sounds and changed a couple of chords here and there and a couple of words here and there and we finally got back together and agreed it was the right thing. The one main thing that I liked about it was that it was not a preaching song because the last thing I want to do is be told to do something. So the idea was to relay issues and problems that were going on but in a reflective tone. So it was basically from a reflective point of view on my behalf looking at the world and seeing how sad it makes me feel as a person. Hopefully when the listener hears it he'll relate to that sadness within himself and say, "I feel the same way as that and maybe I can do something about it." So that's the aim.

Who's playing slide guitar on the record, it sounds like George Harrison.

No, it's not George. I had originally done the slide solo and Bob (Ezrin) and I thought that it's that kind of a song, why don't we at least see if George would even consider it. So we sent the tapes over but unfortunately he was with Eric Clapton just after his son died so it was a very tragic point in their lives. And George was not that focused, why should he be? But he did throw down a couple of ideas. So what we did was we took 3/4 of my solo, a 1/4 of George's solo and threw them in a pot and had someone else play it who was Steve Hunter, a brilliant guitarist who's played with Alice Cooper and Lou Reed.

Can you recount some of the stranger interpretations of your music by fans?

The majority has been "Is this about your dad?" And the majority is not. I don't know why people think I sit around the house and constantly think about Dad all the time. So it's very strange that they should think that or that I still communicate or have close relationships with the Beatles. I mean they were Dad's friends. They were acquaintances. I knew them when I was three years old. What do they want? "So are the Beatles getting back together?" I don't bloody know! Ask them! "Well, are you going to be part of them?" How could I be part of them? The Beatles were in the past and I'm in the present and the future. It's a different story these days. So on and on it goes.

What are your thoughts on Lenny Kravitz having major success aping your father's musical style?

I had a go at him for that. Oh my god, if I used that much influence, watch out. He's a very sweet guy. I had a couple of drinks with him one evening. He invited me to come to his room and have a chat and have a drink which I did but a lot later than he asked me to. And I walked in and I had a serious go at him. I said, "What is going on with you?" I said, "Yeah, it's all right using influence but where are you in all of this?" It's mainly influence and it's none of his own personal identity. Even the vocal riffs and everything else.

BRYAN ADAMS

BRYAN ADAMS   PHOTO COURTESY: ANDREW CATLIN/A & M RECORDS

One of the Eighties most successful artists, Bryan Adams captivated the music world with his gutsy blue-collar evocations of life and love in the real world. A major Beatles fan, Adams holds the distinction of playing with all three surviving Beatles at successive "Prince's Trust" benefit galas. We caught up with the Canadian sensation where he raved about the impact The Fab Four continues to have on his music.

What did the Beatles music mean to you?

I wrote a lot of my songs with Jim Vallance who is my partner for tunes and I think we were pretty much influenced by Lennon and McCartney because of their ability to keep a good melody and lyric in context. Without a question, no doubt, the best songwriting team ever.

How about a favorite Beatles song?

It's hard to pick my favorite Beatles tune because there's so many good ones but I'll say "I Am The Walrus" because it was so obscure. I don't know. There's just something about that song and the cello arrangement that I really dig. When we were playing in bar bands, we played Beatles songs until the roof caved in. But I've never actually recorded any. Everyone still does them.

BADFINGER

L-R: MIKE GIBBINS, PETE HAM, TOM EVANS & JOEY MOLLAND   COURTESY: APPLE CORPS, LTD.

With an infectiously melodic sound reminiscent of their idols, The Beatles, Badfinger had their own run of impeccably crafted hit singles including "No Matter What," "Baby Blue," and "Day After Day" throughout the Seventies. Signed to the Fab Four's Apple Records label, Badfinger scored their first smash single with "Come And Get It," a song written and produced by Paul McCartney for the film "The Magic Christian," which featured Ringo Starr. Enjoying a close working relationship with John, Paul, George and Ringo, Badfinger went on to play on both John Lennon's "Imagine" album and George Harrison's "All Things Must Pass" LP. Harrison also produced several tracks on the group's "Straight Up" record. Lead guitarist Joey Molland and drummer Mike Gibbins recall how their own group was profoundly influenced by the collective genius of The Beatles.

Why have you reformed Badfinger?

Joey Molland: Money. We finally got our money. In 1974, all our money was stopped. Actually, what we did was we went to Apple and said, "Don't pay any more royalties out 'cause it's all getting ripped off." And they said, "Okay." They held onto the royalties for a while and they put it into an escrow account with a court in England so we had no access to it. We didn't have any money for years. All our royalties, all our wages were in an escrow account. In 1985, we went to court and finally got our money which was real nice and that was why we put the band together again.

When you were signed to Apple Records, were you aware of the sense of chaos and craziness that was going on at the time?

JM: No. We didn't know anything about that. We were lucky enough through some of our acquaintances to get a tape to them and I think John and Paul or John and George really liked the songs and they signed us. I think George and John actually signed the contracts with us. George gave us a great deal and we went on to make our records.

We heard that John and Paul both came up with names for the band. Is that true?

JM: Yeah. Paul wanted to call the group "Mama's Boys". John wanted to called the group "The Pricks" more like Grand Prix, you know P-r-i-x. Great, John, knockout. (laughs) It was Neil Aspinall who actually thought of Badfinger.

There's a story going around that the working title for "With A Little Help From My Friends" was "Badfinger Boogie."

JM: Yeah, I've heard that. That was the name of the record that Neil must have got the name of the band from because he had the actual record "Badfinger Boogie." And that's how it turned out where we got the name from.

When did you realize that Badfinger had first made it in as a group?

JM: After "No Matter What" and the album "No Dice"

came out, and "No Matter What" was a big hit for us. It was our first self-penned hit record. Apple didn't want to release it by the way. Peter (Ham) had written the song and we said "Put this out as the next single," and they said, "No. It's not good enough, it won't make it." But it did make it. They put it out and it was a big smash hit. "No Dice" came out and we got all those great reviews and that's when I thought the band really made it. They started talking about us not the Beatles in our reviews. Mal Evans, he was the roadie for The Beatles and he produced "No Matter What." He took a real interest in the group and he would always come out to the house and see if we were doing okay. Great guy, big gentle giant. Lovely fellow. Perfect roadie for the band. Big, nobody could threaten you. Just a really nice and kind fella. Everybody loved him, he was a knockout guy. He got shot in Los Angeles. He'd tell us stories about the Boston concert where the Beatles left all their clothes at the airport. This was like '64 or '65, Boston Garden, sold out. The Beatles had arrived but no clothes. They got their jeans on, their scruff T-shirts. They can't go on. Mal calls up the police and they cleared the freeways. All the lights had switched to green right back to the airport. They get the flight.....this is all in twenty minutes from Boston Garden to Logan Field back to Boston Garden. The Beatles got their clothes and the show was saved. (laughs)

How did Paul come to contribute the song "Come And Get It" to the band?

JM: We had the record "Maybe Tomorrow" by the Iveys out in America and it was a minor hit for us. Paul got the job writing the music for "The Magic Christian" and he wrote "Come And Get It" and he thought this would be a good song for the Iveys to do. They'll have a hit with it, it'll get them on their way, it'll be good for Apple. It's good for you, good for me. Let's do it. (laughs)

There's a great demo floating around on bootlegs of Paul doing "Come And Get It." Have you heard it?

JM: Yeah, it's identical. Badfinger did the identical arrangement. That's why Paul made the demo, "this is how it goes. Do it like this and it'll be a hit record." And it was a hit record.

Tell us about "Without You," a song that was a smash hit for Harry Nilsson.

JM: It's on the "No Dice" album. Peter had the verse and Tommy had the chorus and we just stuck them together. We didn't really think of it seriously as a song. We thought it's a ballad but there's much better songs on the record. But it was the number one song around the world.

Badfinger had the unique distinction of working with all four Beatles.

JM: They all knew exactly what they were doing. We worked with John, we worked with George, Ringo, Paul. All of them know exactly what they're doing in the studio at any given time. I mean records they made, all the time they spent in the studio besides being as creative as they are.

Badfinger had quite a connection with George Harrison. He produced "Straight Up" and you played on his "All Things Must Pass" album.

JM: We played on all of it. What he did was he got about 23 musicians on the album. He had them all there, all day. What we'd do is two or three songs a day. I don't know whether he used all the instrumentation on every track. I remember we played on every song. "Watch out now"...("Beware Of Darkness") All that stuff. "My Sweet Lord," we played all the rhythm guitars. Phil Spector wasn't in charge. George was really in charge. We'd all get there about noon. We'd get our guitars and tune up and stuff and then George would play us a song and we'd all learn it right away. He'd come and play it for you, show you the chords, and we'd learn it. Then we'd go over it once or twice and then we'd record it. It was just like a work a day atmosphere. It wasn't like this super buzz going on. It was just a work a day thing. There were some great bits like the Apple jam. They were the kind of fun times. They were added as an afterthought. It was a lot of fun.

We're curious about one of the jams... "I Remember Jeep." What was that named after?

JM: It was named after the Jeep character in "Popeye." The guy that goes through the walls and everything, yeah. (laughs) I think that's what it was about though I never said to George what this song "Jeep" is about, so I don't know.

What did you think of George as a player?

JM: He's a lot better than I thought. I thought he was really good but he's a lot better than I thought. Did you see the Carl Perkins special? Did you see the solo he played on "Blue Suede Shoes?" It was the original solo, the guy played the note for note solo. That's what I loved about George. He did his homework.

Any recollections of playing The Concert For Bangladesh?

JM: We were doing the "Straight Up" album with George and we did about four or five songs. The Bangla Desh thing happened, the crisis. remember when they had the flood and millions of people died? George got totally into it and right away Ravi Shankar called up and said, "This is a disaster. Can you do anything?" George came to us and he said, "I've got to go and do this thing so I'm gonna get one of my friends to come over and finish the album." He was real nice. Todd Rundgren came in and he did the rest of the album. Anyway, it was nice of George to invite us to do the concert. It was a great thrill. Bob Dylan came down and he was fabulous. That's the memories that stick out in my head of Bob Dylan arriving and Eric Clapton on Saturday. We played all those songs. It was just the band at the Garden doing a dress rehearsal. What a fabulous time.

Speaking of "Straight Up," we spoke with Todd Rundgren and he said that he produced "Day After Day," not George Harrison. What's the real story?

JM: George produced it and Todd mixed it. And that's an actual fact. He had absolutely nothing to do with the recording, absolutely nothing to do with the recording!

Mike Gibbins: As far as the drums go on that record, the

original backing track had the drums played the same but had a different sound. The sound sucked, right. Todd came in and said, "It's great but the drums sound like shit. Play the same stuff again, exactly the same and we'll double-track it."

JM: Did you do that?

MG: Yeah, he said, "It's not what you're playing. It's the sound of the drums." I redid the drums man, note-for-note.

When you hear "Day After Day" on the radio today, what goes through your mind?

MG: I think, there's another fifteen dollars! (laughs)

Have you heard Joe Jackson's "Breaking Us In Two" which sounds exactly like "Day After Day?"

JM: Yeah. "Remember, ooh-ooh, ooh" (imitates song's melody) I wished him all the best with it. If it's a hit for us, it'll be a hit for Joe. That's okay. (laughs)

Tell me about one of the group's most explosive and dynamic records, "Baby Blue."

JM: Knockout record, a real beat group record. It sounds like the band as well. It sounds more like the group than "Day After Day."

Badfinger played on two tracks on John Lennon's "Imagine" album, "Jealous Guy" and "I Don't Want To Be A Soldier."

JM: It was great. John was fabulous. He was my hero. When I saw him come in the room there, we'd already hung around his house and looked at all his stuff. It was great. He had this little magic pad, a roomful of Dr. Pepper, a secret billiard room, a Wurlitzer jukebox in the kitchen with all the great records like Elvis' "Treat Me Nice," "Roll Over Beethoven." No Beatle records. The chicks hanging around making coffee and tea. The studio in the back with all his guitars hanging on the wall. I thought, 'these are actually Johnny Lennon's guitars right here.' And then he came in. It was eleven o'clock at night and he'd just got out of bed. He comes in with Yoko, sits on the stool, tells Jim Keltner to play the beat and says "this is the first song" and he played "Jealous Guy." And there's John Lennon, you know, singing in my ears and I thought I was gonna fucking die! I came out of the booth and sat right down on the floor in front of him. And I was just kind of ga-ga. I couldn't believe this was John and I could actually touch him. And he's singing "Jealous Guy" and it was just great. We learned the chords. It was masterful, just fabulous. A real high spot.

When did the rot set in for Badfinger?

JM: The band started getting pissed because we had these guys come in telling us how to play. Actually telling us about words to songs. That's the last thing that any group needs that's successful. They don't need anybody coming in messing with their music, messing with their words, messing with their people with their characters, they don't need that. Musicians need their freedom. Once you get successful at what you do, nobody should ever fuck with you at all. But they do, and they came around and I hated it. The beginning of the end of the band right there.

What led to Pete Ham's tragic demise?

JM: After I left the band in November '74, I went straight to America. The band went back into the studio...Peter (Ham), and Tommy (Evans), Mike (Gibbins) and the keyboard player Bob Jackson for Warners and did an album called "Head Start" and Warners wouldn't release it. And it was shortly after that where Pete found himself in a situation where he couldn't deal with it anymore and he hung himself. That was really when the band died right there, in between me leaving and Pete dying.

How would you like Badfinger to be remembered?

JM: Well I think we're a great example of what bands should not do. The way bands should not go about making records and doing their business. Badfinger is a perfect example. (laughs)

ROGER EBERT

ROGER EBERT PHOTO COURTESY: DAVID WAGENNAR

hen you think of film critics, none are more recognizable and revered than Gene Siskel and Roger Ebert, the Laurel & Hardy of movie critics. Each week, millions of movie buffs tune into Siskel & Ebert's syndicated TV show for their incisive comments on the latest big screen fare. A Pulitzer Prize winner and Beatle fan, Roger Ebert shares his critical evaluations of The Beatles' now legendary films, "A Hard Day's Night" and "Help."

Give us your own critical assessment of the Beatles' film legacy.

"A Hard Day's Night" was a good movie. But apart from anything else what "A Hard Day's Night" made out of the Beatles were genuine stars. A star changes our idea of how we think about the star and how we think about ourselves. And I believe that by 1965, people in this country and England were behaving and dressing differently because of the Beatles. "Help" is a fun movie—it's not as good as "A Hard Day's Night." "Yellow Submarine" is a good animated film, but of course you don't really get another Beatles film then after "Help." There's "Let it Be" which was sort of a farewell to the Beatles. But the two great Beatles films are "A Hard Day's Night" and "Help."

HEART-NANCY WILSON

L-R: ANN WILSON AND NANCY WILSON OF HEART
PHOTO COURTESY: LANCE MERCER/CAPITOL RECORDS

a self-confessed Beatlemaniac, Heart's guitar slinging beauty Nancy Wilson, along with Stevie Nicks, Chrissie Hynde and Bonnie Raitt, helped pioneer the role of females in rock. Since their formation in 1974, Heart has enjoyed two decades paved with gold and platinum records. Sisters Ann and Nancy are first generation Beatle fans and here Nancy recalls seeing the band first-hand in their hometown of Seattle in August 1966.

We understand that John Lennon is your musical hero.

He was probably so much my idol all through those years, the Beatles years. We were definitely motivated by them and inspired by them to do what we do today. And the whole culture was. If you missed anything, it was the Sixties.

(laughs) But Lennon was like such a hilarious, brilliant, sarcastic, cutting guy who saw through the bullshit. He was kind of this rogue from Liverpool who really had an eye for hypocrisy. And he wasn't afraid to look like a fool to stand up for what he believed. Especially later in the 70's with Yoko. You know, by press standards, by media standards, probably made total idiots of themselves but they made a splash. And of course after his death, it was in context what he had done. Unfortunately, it was only then that people got it.

Didn't you almost meet McCartney on his last tour?

We had a chance to meet him when he played Seattle. We could have pushed it but we didn't because we know what it's like when you play a show and if there's already a lot of chaos. We kind of chickened out basically! (laughs) We're really great, great fans and we respect what he does.

We're sure Paul would love to meet you.

Hey, we got Linda's cookbook! (laughs) We got it over in London. It's pretty good.

What touched you about The Fab Four?

The Beatles did such amazing groundbreaking musical stuff. They were like one of those very rare bands that don't follow, they were leading. And they were discovering as they went along. They discovered all kinds of musical equipment. Stuff like flangers and phasers that are just totally taken for granted today in sounds and ideas.

Didn't you see The Beatles live?

Oh yeah. We saw them in '66 on their last American tour. And of course, we were in a group then already. I must have been 12. We had our band uniforms on that looked like the Beatles uniforms. They had those khaki high collar military jackets. But we had our khaki jackets and our khaki skirts with our nylons and pumps. Our mom made them for the show.

I understand you still remember where you sat.

It was September 25th, row E, and I can't remember the seat. But it was really like the biggest thrill of thrills. We were just mad at everybody who was screaming so loud 'cause we couldn't hear 'em. 'Cause we were there and we had our binoculars. It was really something. It was really something because back then they'd just play for about a half an hour. They had this tiny little drum riser. We saw their road rider one time, what they asked for in their dressing rooms. And all it was was a drum riser with general specifications. And backstage just some towels, a six pack of Coca-Cola, tea and cigarettes. And that was about it. (laughs)

George Martin in front of Abbey Road Studios, 1993
Photo courtesy: Brian Rasic/Capitol Records

GEORGE MARTIN

he true "fifth" Beatle, producer George Martin was eminently responsible for sculpting and, ultimately, perfecting the band's sound in the recording studio. Martin was a classical musician who had made his mark in the late Fifties producing comedy records for the likes of Peter Sellers and the Goons. Yet he was the perfect productive foil for The Beatles. Here George discusses his musical upbringing and, of course, his work with "The Fab Four."

How did you get started with music?

I was always sort of interested in music even as a kid. We had a piano in the house and I started playing when I was about five years old. I was kind of self-taught. I didn't go to music college or anything like that and I didn't take up music as a career until after I came out of Fleet Air Arm when I hadn't any career to go to. I was advised to take it up because I was good at it, as simple as that.

You've mentioned that your greatest love is classical music yet you've spent most of your life in the pop music industry. Do you see that as coming down from classical music?

Not at all. I started out in recording work actually doing classical music. I was working for a small label and we had to do everything like orchestral music, classical, jazz, Scottish country dance music. Everything. You had to be a jack of all trades and I loved it. I found that recording the so called pop music was much more creative because when you record classical music all you can do is interpret something that's already been there for hundreds of years and so many people have done it before so your interpretation is just another version of the same thing. When you're working in the medium of rock and roll or pop, you actually are building something. It may not be as good but it is more creative.

What were those early days with EMI like?

Well very different from today. When I first went into the studios we were still recording on wax. We weren't recording on tape because it was too unreliable. Would you believe it that when we made records in those days, there was a lathe in the control room which was turned by a falling weight because electric motors weren't steady enough. So that was my sort of beginnings in the record business. Even in the times of the Beatles which was twelve years later, we still only had mono and stereo recordings. We didn't have any multi-track recording at all.

What was the role of the record producer in those days?

He was a kind of manager more than anything else. The word producer wasn't used. In fact, my first title was A&R manager (Artists and Repertoire). The job was basically to look after the artists and make sure they were happy and look after them in the studio. And give them advice about music too and make sure the engineer did his job and book the studio and all the musicians. It was a kind of general fixer.

When you were put in charge of the Parlophone label in 1955, what did you want to do?

Well in one way I was lucky because in those days Parlophone was a nothing label. It was the poor relation of the EMI outfit and we didn't have the advantage of any great catalogs coming from America. I used to look enviously at my brothers across at HMV and Columbia who had RCA/Victor imports and Columbia of America imports. They had people like Elvis Presley, Guy Mitchell, Frankie Laine, Doris Day, and all these kinds of people. I had nothing. I had just our own British market and I had to build it. So it was a marvelous challenge and I couldn't very well go down because we were pretty well down there anyway. (laughs)

You were a pioneer in recording British humor. Did you have a great interest in comedy anyway?

Yeah. I was always sort of fond of dramatics and funny

people. I met up with Peter Ustinoff and made a record which was great fun and I thought it would be a good idea to do more of this. I found when I started making comedy records that it was very difficult because you had to be very very careful with your material before you even went into the studio. So when I started recording Peter Sellers I spent a tremendous amount of time doing the spade work of preparing the ground before we got into the studio, making sure the material was right and how we were going to do it.

You've had a fantastic career as a composer. What are the logistics of writing a piece?

When people say writing music they think of composing music which isn't necessarily the same thing. I mean physically putting something down on paper isn't necessarily. Someone like Paul McCartney for example doesn't write music. He thinks of it and he plays it and he sings it and he performs it and he remembers all that he does as he goes along. And generally to get something good is really quite difficult. As for scoring and that kind of writing music, it's jolly hard work. We haven't really progressed much since Dickens' day.

You wrote film scores for such things as "Yellow Submarine," "A Hard Days Night," and "Live And Let Die." Which do you remember as being the hardest?

The hardest work was... I don't know, I think they were all pretty much the same. That doesn't mean to say they weren't enjoyable because a thing like "Yellow Submarine" was enormously enjoyable because I was given complete free reign. We did that film from start to finish in only a year which is remarkable for an animated film. Disney used to take a minimum of two. We had to work so fast because the money was drying up. And because of that the director said to me, "You'll have to write the music while we're making the film." Normally in animated films, you do the music first and they animate to it rather than the other way around in live-action films. So I would receive from him a half finished reel of film and he'd say, "Have a look at this on your Movieola and write what you think is right for it and we'll sort it out afterwards." So I had a completely blank sheet and I was able to do what I wanted which was very nice, very enjoyable.

Can you remember the first song you ever wrote?

Yeah. (laughs) And if I had a piano I'd play it for you. It was a little piece called "The Spider's Dance" and I was eight years old.

Do you think The Beatles as a group put a special emphasis on composers?

Well I think the success that they generated throughout the world did an awful lot for music and music in this country, and an awful lot for this country too. In America, even to this day people in this country don't really realize what happened in 1963 and 4 in America when we really took America by storm and that opened the floodgates and earned us a tremendous amount of money in visible exports.

How did you come to sign up The Beatles?

I was looking for a group. In 1962, I was running the Parlophone label and I already had a few artists that were doing quite well but I felt that I could do something extra. I heard from a publisher that there was a guy walking around with some tapes that was interesting. He sent me Brian Epstein. Brian Epstein came in and played me a disc of the Beatles and I thought it was moderately interesting and I thought I better have a look at the chaps. I told Brian to bring the boys down to London. He groaned inwardly because as I learned later, it had been his last chance. He'd been around every record company. I spent an afternoon with them in the studios at Abbey Road and I thought they were marvelous and I signed them. I was hooked on them more than their music because at that stage I was not at all convinced that they could write music. But they had something different, you see. They were great people to be with. I learned afterwards that they were great Goon fans and they knew about me so I was pretty famous to them. They were prepared to like me but I certainly were very charmed by them.

Did you often take part musically in Beatles recording sessions?

Oh yes, very much so. Well sometimes I used to play with them but generally I mean obviously I used to organize the music and participate in the arranging and just working generally with them. It was a team, the five of us were fairly equal people in the studio. Certainly to begin with, I used to control them more but later on (laughing) they controlled me as they got more successful. But we always worked very closely together.

If you had to give in a nutshell the reason for "Beatlemania" what would it be?

Timing. The world was ready for something and young people were just about to break over the traces and they wanted a kind of symbol of that and the Beatles happened to be coming along at the right time. Having said that, I think it's unlikely that we'll get such a combination of talents again in a short space of time because John Lennon and Paul McCartney were incredibly talented people. I mean Paul still is. Extraordinarily talented songwriters. And for the two of them to get together in itself was amazing but to have them joined by George and Ringo, tremendous personalities in their own right, it was invincible looking back on it. It's extraordinarily lucky that they ever came together and I was very lucky that I joined them too.

Were there times in the early days that you felt The Beatles wouldn't make it?

With them? No. Never. When I first saw them, I knew that there was something there. When we made the first record I knew that it wasn't going to be a hit. But I knew all I had to do was find the right song and I would have a big hit with them. I didn't know at that stage that they could write it. But when they came along with "Please Please Me," I knew they could.

How are hits made? How do you plug a record?

Well again nowadays it's different from what it was in those days. In those early days, television was beginning to mean something. I think our first big break with "Please Please Me" came when we got a "Ready Steady Go" performance which was done by Dick James. He was plugging for us at the time and became the Beatles publisher. And he fixed it with Phil Jones who's now very big in television and he was the producer of that particular show. And that helped enormously. And today there's so much competition, there's so many records that are good that you have to have a combined forces assault from all directions...land, sea, and air. You've got to really go for television, you've got to go to radio, you've got to go to advertising on buses even and posters and so on. It really is a massive thing to do now, to break someone new.

Which is more exciting getting to the top of the charts in Britain or the U.S.?

Well obviously the U.S. because it's such a bigger market. Over the past ten or fifteen years, I've concentrated on America. The population is four times as high than in Britain but the record buying population are much larger than that.

GEORGE HARRISON & GEORGE MARTIN REUNITED INSIDE ABBEY ROAD STUDIO TWO, SEPTEMBER 1993
PHOTO COURTESY: BRIAN RASIC/CAPITOL RECORDS

What do you think The Beatles did for Britain's image in the States?

They put Britain on the American map. If you stop anybody in America and ask them to say one thing that will make you think of Britain. And they'll say "Beatles."

Still?

Still. It's legendary.

What was your most memorable experience being on the road with The Beatles?

New York, the first time they hit America was amazing because I wasn't prepared for the sight of middle-aged men wearing Beatle wigs walking down Fifth Avenue. And also I was astonished to find that every radio station in the New York area was playing a Beatles record. You could not turn the dial and not find a Beatles record being played. It was absolute saturation. Absolutely amazing, I didn't believe it.

What are your thoughts on The Beatles' compilation albums?

Well this is all done by people who own the original masters, the record company, and you can't blame them I suppose for milking the cow a little bit further. They keep digging them up and repackaging them and putting out "Beatle Love Songs" and "Beatle Rock n' Roll" and "Complete Beatles" and so on. In fact, I had a call from a friend of mine in the States the other day saying that you could buy the complete works of the Beatles, all the music, and the lyrics and the records, as one package now for 350 dollars and should he do it? And I said, "No. For heaven's sake don't, that's an awful waste of money." (laughs)

What are your feelings about unreleased Beatles material being issued?

Well there's very little. There's very little unreleased material at all and what there is isn't very good. They still haven't put out the record I made of "How Do You Do It?"

which we didn't release. That was the second thing I did after "Love Me Do." I made it with Gerry and The Pacemakers instead and that was quite good. But the rest of the stuff is pretty much rubbish, I'm afraid.

How about the BBC recordings?

Well that's not records you see. That's like anybody doing a broadcast and you can tape that. There's a lot of bootlegs of that going around and some of it is quite good.

Were there two versions of "Strawberry Fields?"

We did actually record it first of all in a fairly heavy way with fairly heavy rock drumming from Ringo which worked out fine but it wasn't really the way I saw it, but I didn't confess to that until John came to me and said, "I'd like to do it again." We'd never recut a title before. He said, "Would you mind if we had another go at it?" And I said, "Well, fine. I'll go along with that, I didn't quite see it that way." So we went and made another record and this time I did a score for it. I did some cellos and trumpets. After that session, John said, "Well, that's fine." And after a couple of days he rang me again and said, "Look, I still like a bit of the first one. Can't we put the two together?" And I said, "Well, there's only two problems. One is that they're a semi-tone apart in pitch and they're also different tempos. And he said, "Go on, you can fix it!" But fortunately the errors of speed and pitch were the right way around. The sharper one was actually faster than the sharper one so I was able to vari-speed the recording and cut the two together.

Weren't there two versions of "Love Me Do" as well?

Yes. But the distinguishing factor there was very small. There's tambourine on one which Ringo is playing and on another one Ringo's playing drums. The one with him playing drums was a big hit. I think the one with the tambourine was issued on the LP.

If you had to choose one Beatles hit which was your favorite, what would it be?

People keep asking me this if I've got a favorite song but I genuinely answer that I haven't got a favorite, I've got a lot of favorites. But I think if I had to choose a double-sided single out of all the singles we issued I would choose "Strawberry Fields" and "Penny Lane" because they are the epitome of John and Paul. I think they're marvelous tracks.

A lot of people still cite "Sgt. Pepper" as the greatest rock album of all time. What makes it so unique?

It was different from anything we'd done before. When we were making it I thought maybe we were being a bit pretentious and I was a little bit worried about that but It was great fun to do because we were letting our hair down and we weren't going to anybody for permission. We just did what we thought was right. And it was very creative in the studio and great fun. But when it came out I was astonished to find that people were with us on it. I thought we'd kicked over the traces a little bit too much. But it was great.

Was it hard making it on four-track?

It was difficult. But the only difficulty there was keeping your head and remembering what you had to do for the future. When you're bouncing one four-track to another you have to remember how much space we're going to lose and what the balance will be like when the drums merge into the guitars because once you did that you're fixed. But that's just the discipline and experience of recording that made me do that. If it had been done on multi-track it would have been easier.

How has the music business changed since you began?

We've talked about the differences in technology and of course there's much more competition now. When I started in the business there were probably only twelve people like me in the whole country making records. Now it seems that every third person I meet is a record producer (laughs) or at least trying to be one. So the whole thing has become much more pervasive. I was lucky to be there at the beginning therefore it would be very difficult to start at the bottom and work your way up now. I would be horrified if I had to do it now.

Who do you regard as your fellow trailblazers in production?

There's lots of great producers not only in this country but in America. One of my dearest friends is Quincy Jones and he's great at producing records. And although we've crossed swords in the past, there have been some great people like Phil Spector who made some marvelous records. And in this country is a great young talent, Martin Rushent, who produced a lot of hits with Human League. Chris Thomas, who is one of my protégés, is a very, very good producer. It would be invidious to go on with names because I can't remember them all. (laughs)

CHEAP TRICK

CLOCKWISE FROM TOP: RICK NIELSEN, BUN E. CARLOS, TOM PETERSSON & ROBIN ZANDER   PHOTO COURTESY: JIM HOUGHTEN/EPIC RECORDS

Cheap Trick are well known for both the zany antics and superb musicianship of their lead guitarist and chief songwriter, Rick Nielsen. Rick shares some of his fond recollections of his time spent in the studio with both John Lennon and the legendary "fifth" Beatle, George Martin.

Why do you think The Beatles are still so popular?

It's because of all the good stuff. Music hasn't really changed that much if you think about it. "Helter Skelter"...that kind of stuff. Songs as topical today and still sound just as good. It was pretty honest stuff. They're not great players but they have that emotion.

You and Bun E. Carlos played on the "Double Fantasy" sessions. Didn't Lennon think you were one of The Bowery Boys?

No. (laughs) When I got to the studio and when Lennon came in he said, "Oh, it's you." He'd heard from Jack Douglas who got us involved with that. He thought I was from "Ozzie and Harriet," that's what I think it was. He didn't think I was from The Bowery Boys. He knew who we were then. You know he'd say, "I've got Bun E. Carlos." He probably thought he was Carlos Alomar for all I know. After that he knew who I was and we got along real well. I got to play on a couple of songs ("I'm Losing You"/"I'm Movin' On") and we came back a second time after we got back from Japan, 'cause that was August 12, 1980. It was cool. I gave him my string-bender, a Fender electric guitar. I got it back three years later from Jack Douglas who got it back from them. Also I had Hamer make me a guitar that I gave to John and I think Sean or Julian has it.

Were you afforded creative freedom during the sessions?

Yeah. They gave us chord charts so we knew the lengths and the widths of the songs. Basically I played what I did. Earl Slick copied my licks. Maybe someday the original version will come out. Andy Newmark copied Bun E.'s stuff. And when I was there Lennon said, "Gee, I wish I had had you on "Cold Turkey" 'cause Clapton choked." You get stuck doing that one riff over and over although I always thought that sounded cool. Lennon wanted it more like what I was doing in the studio there.

What was John like as a rhythm guitarist?

He was a real good rhythm player. When he played leads, they were sloppy but that was cool...that attitude. He had it. He was a songwriter. I think of myself as a songwriter not an ace virtuoso guitar guy. I happen to play guitar. He was cool to work with. He was great.

Have you had any encounters with the other Beatles?

McCartney almost bought a guitar I had. (the guitar—a left-handed Gibson Les Paul was later bought by Paul several months after this interview for use on his 1989-90 world tour) We were gonna have dinner together with George Martin but we didn't. A song that Robin Zander wrote and he wants me to do some lyrics for is going to George Harrison. I was also asked to produce one half of Ringo's solo record and that didn't happen too. A lot of stuff that I've been asked to do that hasn't happened. Not always my fault, sometimes just timing is bad and that's usually what happens.

George Martin produced Cheap Trick's "All Shook Up" album. What was it like to work with such a legendary and well respected producer?

George was a gentleman...a great guy. The guy that's done it all. He could retire...he doesn't need to do anything. I just saw him again about a year ago. He's one of the best producers around. He's a producer and a musician. A lot of producers are not real good musicians. George Martin could sit down and play the piano or score this. You could talk musically with him where some of the other guys couldn't. We want this to sound like a steamroller running over a chicken.

Did he share any neat Beatles stories with you?

Oh yeah, a lot of funny stuff. One thing I remember is that Yoko was sick and John wouldn't sing the vocal without her in the bed. They rolled the bed in the studio and he's holding her hand while singing the song. (laughs) Well I guess she's all right. I guess it worked.

In concert you've played a special Beatles guitar.

It was just a Hamer guitar with The Beatles on it. When we did "Day Tripper" and I put the dates on it when the Beatles' "Day Tripper" was released and when ours was released. It just had some faces of the Beatles and that's it. I had it made because I get so many guitars made for the day of the week or flavor of the month. And that was the flavor of the month that time.

You did a cover of The Beatles' "Magical Mystery Tour."

I think it's the soundtrack for something. Michael Jackson has something to do with it. It sounds like Cheap Trick. It's not us trying to do a Beatles song and make it sound like Cheap Trick. It's neat. I'm surprised that we actually did it as good as we did.

Cheap Trick are often compared to The Beatles. Can you understand the comparisons?

I liked the melodic part of The Beatles and the heavy part of The Beatles. That stuff I liked a lot. That's probably why we get those comparisons. It's not a Beatles rip off, it's an attitude of music.